WE WALK
BESIDE YOU
ALWAYS

About the Author

Bridget Benson (United Kingdom) was born in County Mayo on the west coast of Ireland. A clairvoyant medium, Bridget conducts public and private readings, appears at charity events, and uses her gift to help with police investigations. She has been a guest on numerous British television and radio programs. Visit Bridget online at www .bridgetbenson.com.

BRIDGET BENSON

WE WALK
BESIDE YOU
ALWAYS

Comforting messages from your
loved ones in the afterlife

Llewellyn Publications
Woodbury, Minnesota

FIRST EDITION
First Printing, 2014

Cover art: iStockphoto.com/12370555/©DeepGreen,
        iStockphoto.com/18140699/©Jeja
Cover design by Maria Garbe
Editing by Connie Hill

Llewellyn Publications is a registered trademark of Llewellyn Worldwide Ltd.

Library of Congress Cataloging-in-Publication Data (Pending)
ISBN: 978-0-7387-3749-2

Llewellyn Worldwide Ltd. does not participate in, endorse, or have any authority or responsibility concerning private business transactions between our authors and the public.

All mail addressed to the author is forwarded but the publisher cannot, unless specifically instructed by the author, give out an address or phone number.

Any Internet references contained in this work are current at publication time, but the publisher cannot guarantee that a specific location will continue to be maintained. Please refer to the publisher's website for links to authors' websites and other sources.

Llewellyn Publications
A Division of Llewellyn Worldwide Ltd.
2143 Wooddale Drive
Woodbury, MN 55125-2989
www.llewellyn.com

Printed in the United States of America

Other books by Bridget Benson

When Tomorrow Speaks to Me

Dedication

There are so many people that I think of to dedicate this book to:

Most of all, I want to thank God for the beautiful gift that he has given me so that I am able to unite our two worlds together, bringing love, reassurance, and comfort to all those that I am privileged to meet throughout this world.

To my husband, Kenn. My children: Mathew, Elizabeth, and Marcus; my grandson, Lennon; and my beautiful new grandson, Kenny, who was born on July 4, 2012. Thanks for your love and support, which I need too. I hope I have left you all a legacy for the next generation.

A special thanks also to Julie Beaumont, my personal assistant, who has spent so many hours getting this book together.

I know that I have made my late parents, Charles and Bridget O'Malley, very happy and proud. Without them I would not be who I am today.

May God continue to bless us with the knowledge that we will all be reunited one day.

Acknowledgments

I wish to give special thanks and much gratitude to Marilou Trask-Curtin, a published author, screenwriter, and playwright, for all her help and support in the writing of this book.

My loved ones in the spirit world answered my prayers to find the best person to help write this book for me and I am truly grateful.

I would like to thank everyone mentioned in my book and also thank Llewellyn Publications for once again accepting and publishing this book. My wish is that it reaches as many people as possible and that whatever they are experiencing, they can be reassured that even though our loved ones can be called back home at any time, they really never leave our side and they walk beside us always.

Contents

Foreword

The first time I met Bridget Benson was when my daughter, Nicola, was about four years old. I had a friend named Nuala, whose sister had come over from Ireland. They were both going to see Bridget for a reading, so I offered to drive them there.

When we arrived, Bridget invited me inside to wait for Nuala and her sister. I walked in with Nicola, who was busy chatting away. Bridget seemed taken aback at this little person with blonde, curly hair. Nicola was equally smitten with Bridget's dog, Benson, and her two lovely cats.

Bridget made us comfortable with a cup of tea and some biscuits. When my friends went in to have their readings Nicola, being Nicola, wanted to know what they were doing and why we couldn't go into the room with them. I told her that they had just gone into the "Posh Room."

When my friends had had their readings, I felt compelled to go and speak with Bridget about Nicola. I knew that there was something wrong with my daughter at that time but didn't have a diagnosis yet and I felt I needed to know about her future. I had no idea of what to expect as I had never been to anything like this before.

Bridget told me how Nicola was feeling. She said that Nicola was always falling over and how much she wished that she could just play like all the other children. Although I was upset, I came out of the room with a smile on my face.

Nicola was then determined to have a look at this "Posh Room" and in she went to see Bridget.

When Nicola came out I could not believe what she said to me. She had told Bridget that all she wanted was to be able to play like all the other children did. I was shocked that she had repeated exactly what Bridget had already told me.

I gave Nicola the money to give to Bridget to pay for my reading but Bridget told Nicola to keep it and buy herself something nice with it. Nicola's face was a picture as she loved the feel of money. This gesture on Bridget's part had made Nicola's day.

We all said our goodbyes, but as we got to the front door Bridget took me to one side and said that she felt she couldn't see Nicola again. She could see that Nicola would end up in a wheelchair, and it was too upsetting for her to know that. I accepted what Bridget had said and we left.

A few years later Nicola would be diagnosed with a very rare genetic disease, giant axonal neuropathy, that is always fatal. At that time I was aware of only two other girls who had also been diagnosed with the condition: one in Scotland and the other in the United States.

The next time we met Bridget was at the Piece Hall in Halifax for Irish Day. My husband, Dave, myself, and Nicola were there. It was a lovely sunny day and Nicola was in her special chair, which helped us to get her around more easily. The place was packed with people, but amazingly Nicola spotted Bridget in the vast crowd. We went over to her and Bridget couldn't believe that, of all the thousands of people in the crowd, we were the last people she thought she would bump into.

We met Bridget's husband, Kenn, who was a lovely man. During the time we chatted, I was astounded to find out how much Bridget and I had in common. We both were called Bridget, both bubbly Geminis, and we were even wearing identical rings!

After this meeting, Bridget and I kept in touch by telephone and our two families became very close. We would always be invited to any party that Bridget held for her family and they were always a part of our family celebrations. Bridget often came over with Kenn to the house to see Nicola, who was very ill at the time. My husband did not believe in anything spiritual so Bridget offered to give him a reading for his fortieth birthday. He couldn't believe what she knew and what she told him!

Bridget continued to keep in touch with us, wanting to know how Nicola was doing. She would telephone and text and Nicola even used to call Bridget herself. Whenever Nicola was ill, Bridget would come over to the house to visit her. Nicola always loved to see Kenn, Bridget, and her children, Mathew, Elizabeth, and Marcus. Nicola also had fond memories of our visit to Ireland to meet Bridget and her family for St. Patrick's Day. There had also been a chance to meet Bridget's friends at the Copper Beech, and while there everyone had made us feel so welcome that we felt as if we were also a part of Bridget's family.

I didn't, during those early years of our friendship, talk to Bridget about Nicola's condition all of the time as I didn't want Bridget to feel that the friendship was just about Nicola, even though Bridget reassured me that it didn't matter what we talked about as she would always be there for me. Sometimes I would talk to Bridget about what it would be like for me when Nicola's time to pass came and how it would affect my husband, Dave, and my son, Gary, and all the family. Even though I knew that Nicola's condition would eventually take her to spirit, I kept putting this to the back of my mind. I was very thankful that I had met someone who had direct contact with the spirit world.

I have known Bridget now for nineteen years and I feel that our meeting her and her family was fate—I do not believe in coincidence. Bridget was meant to be a part of Nicola's life and our lives as well. I am sure that we were guided the day that I brought my friends to Bridget's house for their reading. Our families continue to be in touch to this day and even though Nicola has passed she still sends messages through Bridget to me and my family. Nicola is aware of all my needs and always reassures me, when I need it most, that she is well and very much enjoying her new life. Nicola remains a very big part of all our family celebrations because she is the one who brought us all together in the first place and we always remember and give thanks for that.

I cannot thank Bridget enough for the love, support, and comfort she has given to me and my family and to Nicola.

—Breege Holmes
January 2013

Introduction

I know that death is not the end, because since I was three years of age I have been in contact with those who have passed over into spirit. This knowledge and remarkable gift was something I would find that I shared with my great-aunt Bridget, my father, and my mother. Even though I thought that my brothers and sisters could all see and feel what I could, I later found out that this was not true. This fact was made known to me when I had my first encounter with a spirit at age three. Having the ability to speak to spirits was something that set me apart from others in my family who did not share this talent or understand it. It also set me apart from my schoolmates when I was growing up in Straide, County Mayo, Ireland.

During the years I was living in Straide in the 1950s, it was a farming community and there we lived a simple life. Our home consisted of a kitchen, a living area, and three small bedrooms. Despite lacking some of the modern conveniences such as electricity, it was a warm and loving home where we all lived a joyful life and I treasure that time deeply. My family in Straide consisted of my mother (also named Bridget), my father, Charles O'Malley, my brothers Charlie, Fergus, Johnnie, William (Billy), Peter, and Oliver, and my sisters Rose and Kathleen. My mother's parents, Grandma Kate and Granddad John, also resided with us. Our great-aunt Bridget lived with us until her death when I was very young. Great-aunt Bridget was a clairvoyant. To me she was incredible because she used to sit on her bed in the same room we children slept in and talk to the spirit of her brother Henry (called Harry) every evening. Before I was born Harry had passed to spirit due to tuberculosis. On one of those nights Harry, who appeared as a very solid, small-statured man, chose to speak to me. While my brothers and sisters slept beside me, I had often stayed awake and watched and listened to his talks with my great-aunt, so when he spoke with me there was nothing at all fearful or scary about it. The ensuing pandemonium that resulted when my siblings awoke one night and found I was communicating with someone they could not see was quite a different thing! My dad had rushed into the room and calmed everyone down and told me that he would speak to me in the morning—but that didn't happen. After everything was quiet I wondered if there might be something wrong with me, but that thought quickly passed as I pondered on my great-aunty being able to see Harry in the room. Some time later I realized that I was truly blessed with a skill my siblings did not share. Because I was *different* from them, these early years were often a confusing and somewhat lonely time for me. There was no one to talk with about what I was experiencing. As time passed, I so wished I could have spoken more with my great-aunt, but, sadly, she developed Alzheimer's just prior to her passing into spirit and her hazy and wandering mind eventually found her not recognizing family members.

When I first saw spirits at three years of age, they appeared to me just as a normal person would. Not at all ethereal but solid beings. Most often it was the clothing that they wore that had me questioning what era they came from. Of course any questions of this sort that I had were answered by Harry, who reassured me that it was perfectly okay if their clothing didn't fit well or that they dressed the same every day.

After that first visit from Harry, my everyday life found me surrounded by spirit friends. Several were very special: Lucy, Mary-Ann (who was Lucy's twin sister), Patrick, and Mary-Ellen. These dear spirit friends were always dressed in different clothes every day and their attire seemed to be of the Victorian era. When the sun was shining the women would wear bonnets. They always had on shoes that looked to me like pixie boots. Patrick wore long shorts that went to his knees. I could always see a great resemblance to my father in Patrick. When I asked Patrick if he was related to me, he said that "We were all related to my father's side of the family" (except, of course, for Harry, who was related to my mother's family). If it was a cold day, Patrick would have on socks that went up to his knees and brown boots. These children in spirit all spoke to me verbally. We shared many good times laughing together. They always wanted to know about my day, and I also wanted to know about theirs. Patrick liked to talk about family history, often going back generations. My friends told me that, as well as helping with my farming chores—something they really enjoyed— there could be the possibility of them being called away to help someone whose needs were greater than mine. It must have been that my need was the greatest because we were together seven days a week. They even accompanied me to school. While there they would do all sorts of mischievous things that usually got me into trouble—but despite that, they always made me feel special. Lucy was the most extra-special to me because we shared the same birthday.

Yet another gift was revealed to me when I was three years of age—the ability to heal.

It happened that one day Dad had a very bad headache. I can recall warming my hands in front of the range that we had in our living room and then placing my hands on Dad's head. I had no foreknowledge of how to do this and there was no one to tell me what to do. Almost immediately Dad said to me, "My headache has gone and it has gone through the strength of the heat coming from your hands." After this it was a regular thing that just happened when I was present with anyone who was in any sort of pain.

I was also able to see the little men or leprechauns, and the fairies would always include me in their dances. It made me feel so happy inside that we were able to share our days and I found myself not wanting to play with Rose, as obviously she could not join in the games in the same way that I could. My dad, who could also see the leprechauns, always commented that my chores were finished before everyone else's and that was because I couldn't wait to be outside with my true spirit friends. I enjoyed their company so much because they were always so kind and never judged or spoke a bad word about anyone. Also, during that time I have memories of the look on my mum's face when she used to say, "Who are you talking to now, Bridget?" I knew then, of course, that my mum was not able to see my friends. I had, however, been reassured by my father and Great-aunt Bridget that I wasn't imagining anything.

Even to this day I still have conversations out loud with my spirit friends because I am either getting information from them or answering questions they are asking me.

My life moved forward. One day when I was still very young, Harry told me from spirit that I would "connect with another world" and that I would be known everywhere by "people of every color, creed, class, and denomination" because of my special gift. This pronouncement sent shivers of anticipation up and down my spine. Even at such a young age I was more than ready to set my foot on the life path that Harry had spoken of.

Of course, it should be noted that Straide was a deeply Catholic community and that such a gift as I had was frowned upon mightily by the church. My communications with Harry often got me into a bit of trouble with my mum, who chided me that I was just imagining Harry and his talks with me. Mum was a very devout Catholic and feared that my special talent might somehow bring shame upon the family.

My father, who was nineteen years older than my mother, was the kindest and most caring man. He was also blessed with the gift of seeing otherworldly beings as well and proved this to me one day when he came up behind me while I was watching some leprechauns at their campfire just outside our kitchen window. When Dad described the little men to me in detail right down to their caps, I knew he was most assuredly a kindred spirit.

Sadly, my dad suffered from diabetes and arthritis. One day when I was in my seventh year and after the passing of my Granny Kate, Harry told me some news I had never wanted to hear—he gently revealed to me that my beloved father would pass away when I was twelve. It was a horrible and crushing message from spirit and it seared my heart with anguish. I wanted so badly to talk to my father about the message from Harry so I waited until I felt that the time was right.

It happened that one day—still during my seventh year —it was my turn to go with my dad to watch the birth of a calf. As it was the early hours of the morning, we were guided by the stars and the moon and an oil lamp that dad was carrying. Dad commented to me about the different sizes of the stars in the sky. I felt then that Dad had an understanding of spirit and this was my opportunity to share with him the message Harry had given me, and my dad confirmed that it was true. My dear father passed into spirit on December 17, 1968. Although Harry never told me about other people dying, I believe he felt it necessary to inform me of my dad's passing so that I would be somewhat prepared for the event and have the ability to communicate with the afterlife.

There is absolutely nothing that can truly prepare one for the loss of a beloved family member—not even having the gift of foreseeing the upcoming event. The passing always removes from your life a physical connection that you have come to rely on. I do still communicate with my father and Harry, and I am constantly grateful for their presence and support and the forever love that sustains me through my days, because, above all, love is eternal and not even death can sever it.

Not long after my dad's passing, the family left Straide and moved to England.

I went on to become a nurse, a wife, and a mother, and then in 1990 I made the decision to leave nursing and become a professional psychic as I could not continue with my nursing due to the constant contact with spirit. Thereafter, I began seeing people from all over the world for private readings at my home and, since February, 2008, from my office, which was built especially for my business. At last I was now doing the work that Harry had predicted for me all those years ago. It has been an extraordinary journey. I do my best to bring comfort and hope into the lives of those who come to share the heartache of their losses with me. I also do my best to reassure them that death is not the end. It is really only the beginning—and this is the reason for this book. It is my way of sharing the hope and comfort I have been able to give to so many as they have faced their own passage to spirit or that of a loved one.

I now offer services in churches and have never charged for them. I give my time freely so that the funds collected can be used for the upkeep of the church. As far as audiences at different venues are concerned, the only time that I wouldn't charge a fee would be if I decided to give my fee, along with any monies raised, to whatever charity/cause the audience was being held for.

My life was and is full of doing what I love—meeting new people, caring for my family, and continuing to be in contact with my beloved father and other loved ones in spirit.

Then, one day in February of 2010, Dad came to me in spirit and told me that I should go and visit my mum, and that I would "notice a big change" in her since I had been away on a trip to Ireland for appointments and readings.

I did as my father suggested and during that visit I found that I was about to face another of the biggest losses in my life—my mum.

CHAPTER 1

My Mum Passes to Spirit

My husband, Kenn, and I called, and Mum was just seated and having a bite to eat. She lifted her head and gave me a lovely smile and asked me where I had been. I told her that I had just returned from Ireland, after having been there for two weeks. The first thing she asked was, "Did you visit your dad's grave, and was everything okay?" I told her that everything was fine and that many had asked how she was and when she would be coming back to Ireland again for a visit. She paused and seemed to think carefully about how she was going to answer me. Then, in a calm voice, she told me that her next visit to Ireland would be her last one, as she was preparing herself for her final journey home.

I did not want to hear these words from Mum, but somehow I knew that what she had told me was the truth and that it was going to happen soon. I held her hand and asked her to go ahead with what she felt was right for me to know. It was most unusual to be talking to Mum about her death as she had never really spoken to me much about the "next world" as she called it, and now here she was telling me all about what was awaiting her on the other side. She also told me that she had been in regular contact with Dad ever since she had said goodbye to him all those years ago and then she informed me that she had the same gift as I did, but that her messages were delivered by "the Lord God Almighty." She also told me that Dad had lately been coming to her in spirit and preparing her for their eternal home together. Mum told me that Dad had spent a great deal of time explaining to her what it was like in heaven. He also told her that he had his own house and had never met anyone else whom he wished to share it with but Mum. This confession on Dad's part gave Mum great joy as she told me that, even though she knew my dad was quite a bit older than her when they first met, she always knew they would be married.

My dad told Mum that he was quite happy with his everyday chores and what was expected of him since he had returned back home to heaven. Other family members had joined him there—my brother Charlie and his wife Anne had gone home in 2008 and 2009 and he had been spending a great deal of time with them. He was also caring for and spending time with Charlie's twin, John Joe, who had passed when he was only two days old. The arrival in heaven of Dad's sisters Mary, Ellen, and Delia, who had relocated to America in the 1940s and whom Dad had not seen since then, was a source of happiness for him as well.

I couldn't help it. My eyes welled up with tears, but I knew I had to hear her story and so I managed to get a grip on my own spiraling emotions and listen to her. Mum went on to tell me that she felt she had fulfilled her time here on earth. She explained that after Dad had died when she was just forty-eight years old, she had struggled with the empty space in her life, although she was so proud to watch her children grow up and become independent—but as each one of us left home, she felt she was needed less and less.

Time seemed to stand still as I sat and listened to Mum talk and two hours slipped by as if they were a few moments, so engrossed was I with her story. I knew she had a great deal more to share with me, but Kenn and I had to leave. As I got up and prepared to go I was overwhelmed with sadness, yet I also had to consider the extraordinary privilege I had been given. I knew that not many daughters were granted the opportunity to sit and talk with their mothers about the topic we had been discussing. I also felt that Mum was feeling a great deal of relief because she had been able to tell me things she wanted me to know. As Kenn and I got ready to leave, I promised Mum that I would be returning to visit her soon.

When we got into our car to drive home, Kenn looked at me and said, "Well, you have been told, straight from the horse's mouth, so you can now start to prepare yourself for what is to come." I never answered him. I just remained silent until I had the time to digest what Mum had said to me.

When I got home, I was greeted by my youngest son, Marcus, who had just got in and was so pleased to see me again. As he hugged me, he also noticed that there was something wrong. I couldn't contain my tears any longer. I told him everything that his grandma had said to me, and he did his best to console me by saying, "Well Mum, Grandma's waited a long time to join Granddad. It must be nearly forty-three years, isn't it, since Granddad passed away? She's also had to watch Uncle Charlie and Aunty Anne pass away before her. Do you remember when Uncle Charlie passed and how she said that she wished she could have changed places with him?"

I told Marcus that I did remember, but that just now I needed time to take all of this on board. He hugged me and went to his room to listen to his music.

I had wanted to ask Marcus where Benson, our black Labrador, was when I heard the familiar sound of those paws bounding down the stairs. He was so happy to see me and nearly licked me to pieces. I cuddled him and he just wouldn't leave my side. In that intuitive way that animals seem to have, it was as if Benson knew and understood that I had just received some bad news and he was doing his best to console and comfort me.

I was totally exhausted and the events of the day were taking their toll.

I knew that I needed to ready myself, both mentally and spiritually, for the difficult time that lay ahead.

The rest of the evening seemed to creep by. Family came and went. I yearned deeply for bedtime to arrive so that I could be in touch with Dad and be able to decide how best to handle Mum's passing. Dad had been in contact with me every day, even if it was just to say a quick "hello" or encourage me in my career. However, with all my time now devoted to reaching out to people from all over the world, I had learned the need to separate my two lives—the professional and the personal—and bedtime gave me the best opportunity if I needed to have a serious discussion with spirit.

That night Dad spoke to me for quite a while and explained as much as possible to me about Mum's impending transition to spirit. I was able to tell him that Mum's final journey home would be a most difficult one as we would have to go through a great deal of red tape to return her body to Ireland. My father said it was my mum's last wish and that it would have to be granted.

We also spoke about how Mum's passing was going to affect my brother Billy, who had lived his entire life with Mum. I knew it would not be an easy time for him. My brother Johnnie also lived with Mum and he was not well. I told Dad, "Everything seems to be coming all at once." He replied, "Yes, it is, Bridget, but you will cope with all this when the time comes and you will have all our help from spirit. Remember the time when Harry told you about my passing and you were only seven years old? I know it's sad and difficult for you, but we felt it right that you should be aware of what is to come and it's good that Mum can talk with you about her transition."

I drifted off to sleep just after mumbling, "Okay."

The next morning was Monday and I awoke to find to my surprise that I had slept quite well. Snow was falling and so my appointments for the day had to be rescheduled. It was as if some benevolent force had granted me the time to spend with Mum and I decided to go and visit her again. When I got there, I could clearly see that things were becoming more difficult for her and also for my two brothers. Mum was having problems sleeping at night and was keeping them both awake. Everyone looked very tired and I could hear Dad telling me that the time had come for a decision to be made regarding Mum's welfare.

I sat down with Mum and explained as best as I could that as a family we felt that she needed more care than we could provide, and would she consider having some respite? Mum looked at me sternly. "No way am I leaving my home. I looked after all of you and now it's time for my family to look after me!" I knew she was right in what she had said, but I also remembered something Dad had told me from spirit that eventually matters would be taken out of my hands. Although Mum had all the love she could ever want in her own home and the help of those who came in to care for her, I could see the effect her decline was having on my two brothers who were caring for Mum on a daily basis around the clock.

After a while, Mum settled down and I stayed to have dinner with her and my brothers Johnnie and Billy. Later that evening my two younger brothers, Peter and Oliver, came to see Mum and they both noticed how much she had deteriorated. There was a discussion about the value of her staying in her own home and it was decided among us that for now it would be okay.

Into the months of February and March things remained the same. I rang Mum every day. My brother Billy would tell me the same stories about Mum over and over again and the sadness and frustration in his voice was so difficult to hear. I constantly wondered what I could do to help ease the burden.

One day I decided it was time to take matters into my own hands and I telephoned Mum's doctor and made an appointment to see him. He was very supportive but he also told me that our mother could only be removed from her home when something happened that would cause a decision to have to be made. In the meantime he arranged for extra help from Social Services.

Once more I felt totally helpless. I loved Mum dearly and wished I could be with her every day but I had a family to look after and a business to run. I was extremely upset and although Dad reassured me that I had his full attention and support, along with that of Harry and my brother Charlie, I still felt that there was no one who truly understood the full impact Mum's forthcoming death was having on all of us.

Although Mum still had eight living children, not everyone, including me, was able to be there to support her and my two brothers. I was now getting daily messages from spirit and I was also visiting Mum on a regular basis. She seemed to be getting worse and her mind was beginning to falter.

One day Mum had a fall from the stairlift my brother Fergus had fitted for her. She had never had a problem before, but this particular day she decided to get up out of the chair before it reached the bottom of the stairs and she fell about three steps. An appointment was made with Mum's doctor who came to visit her. He was unable to prescribe any medication that would help her settle at night. The concern was that any new medicine of that nature could make Mum's condition worse, because by this time she had been diagnosed with vascular dementia. Vascular dementia is a condition where oxygen does not flow freely from the heart to the brain and, therefore, cells are continually dying and not being renewed.

Time went by and at the end of March I received a phone call from Mum's doctor asking me if I could come by her house as he had arranged a meeting with Social Services. Social Services had received a distressing telephone call from my brother, Billy, during the previous evening saying that he couldn't cope anymore.

The welfare of my two brothers was of grave concern. Billy's health was not good and Johnnie was ailing as he came to terms with having colon cancer and surgery.

Mum's doctor now felt that a place needed to be found for her in a safe and secure nursing home that would be able to deal with dementia patients. The doctor made a few phone calls and Mum's health was assessed quickly. Two nurses from The Grange at Rastrick agreed that Mum definitely needed full-time care. In an odd twist of fate, one of those nurses expressed her shock when she saw my mum as Mum had held her as a newborn baby over forty years ago, and now this woman was to care for my mum as Mum had cared for her.

Luckily The Grange at Rastrick had a room available for Mum. It was ideal as it was only down the road from her home and family members and friends could visit her easily.

All the necessary paperwork was completed and it was now left to me and my brother, Fergus, to take Mum to The Grange. It was one of the saddest days of my life because Mum was leaving the home where she had lived for thirty-seven years, and I knew deep in my heart that she would never return.

But there was no turning back.

The decision had been made and, as foretold, matters had been taken out of our hands.

Fergus arrived and I placed a few of Mum's things in a bag.

Mum didn't say a word about leaving her home although she was very much aware of what was happening, probably because she was very weary. She was not aware, as far as I could tell, that she was most likely leaving her home for the last time. She did ask, "Why am I going on my own when I always go everywhere with my family?" She didn't get angry or tearful but I could feel her sadness as if it too were a physical presence. She held my hand and asked me, "Why am I going away?" I tried to explain once more that the family felt that she needed more care than we could give her. "Why, when I have so many people in the family to take care of me?" she asked. I didn't have the heart to tell her that not all of those people—meaning family—could take care of her. She asked if I would be staying with her and I told her that I would. She wanted to know where I would be sleeping and I had no other choice but to lie and tell her that I would be in the room next to hers.

Just before we left Mum's home, she turned back and looked at the photographs of herself and Dad and all the others that were displayed on her cabinet, and she reached out and touched the one of her and Billy that I had given her just a few weeks before. She said to me, "Does Johnnie know that I am going away and are Johnnie and Billy going away?" I reassured her that they did know. I couldn't tell her that Johnnie was upstairs in bed because I felt this would be too much for her to handle. Mum, as always, seemed far more concerned about her family than she did about herself.

On the way to The Grange, Dad came to me and said, "I'm with you all the way, Bridget. Please be strong."

Fergus was overcome with emotion and became so distressed that he couldn't stay with us. He went to wait outside in his car, so I went in alone with Mum to help her get settled.

When Mum got in her room at The Grange, she wondered where she was and I told her again that she was on holiday for two weeks. She did not question this any more, but when she held my hand and gave it a gentle squeeze and put her head down I realized that she knew what was occurring. My heart was breaking. I had promised Mum so many times in the past that I would take care of her; now it was all out of my hands. If Mum felt any fear at all she certainly didn't show it. She faced this event straight on, because she had learned through her life experiences, and especially after losing Dad, that some things are meant to be.

Mum's room was actually quite lovely. To personalize the room we were able to bring photographs and memorabilia from her home. I stayed with her for quite a while. The rest of the family came and voiced their opinion about Mum being in a nursing home; nevertheless, Mum had to stay there for the two weeks as had been arranged. All of the family eventually came to the conclusion that Mum was safer at The Grange than she had been at home.

Some time later Fergus took me home.

Shortly after Mum's placement I had a talk with Billy and explained to him that the staff at The Grange thought it best that he not visit Mum for at least a week so that each of them could get used to their new lifestyle. Billy became very sad at this news and I understood his pain, yet also knew he could now get some much-needed rest.

Kenn and my family reassured me that they believed it was in Mum's best interest to be in the nursing home. My daughter, Elizabeth, even commented that her grandma could now have regular visitors. While she had been living at home with my two brothers, it was almost an intrusion of their privacy when anyone called to visit Mum. My little grandson, Lennon, who was two years old at the time, gave me a big hug. Even though he was so young, he also seemed to notice the sadness throughout the home.

Mum would never stop asking when she could go home.

❦

When night again came I couldn't wait to speak to Dad but before I went to bed I rang the nursing home to check in on Mum. I was told that she was finding it difficult to settle in her new environment and kept asking for Billy and Johnnie. I told them to keep telling her that they were okay. I left my mobile telephone number with them and gave instructions to call me at any time—day or night.

I lay down and awaited Dad's presence.

It wasn't long before our conversation began. This time Dad was accompanied by Harry, who was there to give support to me. "Where would you like me to start, Bridget?" Dad asked. I looked at both of them and said, "I need to know how long Mum has left here before she joins you."

"Not long, Bridget. Soon after her ninetieth birthday," Dad said.

I sighed heavily. Mum's birthday was only three weeks away.

I looked at my father closely. "You look so young, Dad. Will Mum recognize you? How often do you two communicate?"

"Every day," Dad said.

"Does Mum know that it is you?"

"Why wouldn't she? I have to say that she is happy and looking forward to her new life here with me," Dad said.

I asked Harry some questions that I had wondered about. "What do you think about all of this, Harry, and why haven't Granny and Granddad, Charlie, or Great-Aunt Bridget come with you?"

"It would be too much for you to take in," Harry stated simply.

"Alright. Can I ask more questions?"

"Yes," Dad responded.

"When Mum is ready to pass over, who will come for her?"

"I will," Dad said. "Together with Charlie and Anne."

"That's good."

As comforting as this sounded, that my mum would be met by her loved ones after she transitioned to spirit, I knew and felt deep in my heart that neither I nor any of the family wanted to let her go. Why, I wondered, was I feeling like this when I was very much aware of what the spirit world was like, and how Mum would be able to come back to me just as Dad did and be beside me always through all my good and bad times.

I was exhausted, yet I didn't want Dad or Harry to leave. Eventually I drifted off to sleep and dreamt all night of the time when Dad had left us and how I had coped with that loss.

The next morning came and the snow was clearing. My day was a busy one. I called to see Mum in the evening. She seemed more settled, but she told me she wasn't staying there and didn't particularly like mixing with the other residents in the nursing home. This was probably because Mum was always so happy just having her own family around and when the other patients came into her room she felt they were invading her privacy.

We talked about her forthcoming birthday and she looked at me and said, "Am I really ninety?"

"Yes, soon," I replied.

"When is soon?" she asked.

"Your ninetieth birthday is on April second, Mum. It's a Friday and the family has arranged a party for you on Saturday, the third, at the Lane Head Hotel, Brighouse, West

Yorkshire, where you can be with your family and friends. There are also family members coming over from Ireland."

She gave me a lovely smile and just said, "I need to go for my long sleep soon."

I knew exactly what she meant and said, "Okay, Mum, but will you please stay until you have your birthday party?"

"Okay. I'll do that, but then I must go."

◯⁄◯

I left Mum's room and had a word with a staff member, explaining that even though Mum had only been in the nursing home for a short period of time, I could really notice the deterioration in her health. I had also noticed that she was losing weight. I asked what her appetite was like and was reassured that Mum did eat but that she wasn't finishing some of her meals. I was assured that this would be closely monitored.

I was totally drained on every level of my being. That night I had a dream of premonition. In this dream Dad came to me with a message that Mum had had an accident at the home and sustained an injury. Around 5:00 a.m. I received a phone call that confirmed the dream was indeed a reality. Apparently Mum had fallen after coming out of her room without the aid of her walking stick. Mum had simply decided to go for a walkabout, something she would have done at her own home. It was obvious that she had become confused and hadn't realized where she was. The fall had badly bruised her wrist and she was taken to the hospital.

I arrived at the hospital with Kenn and noticed that Mum's right wrist was swollen and she was also complaining of pain in her hip. I rang my brother Oliver and he joined us at the hospital. Oliver was clearly upset about Mum's fall, but he also was very much aware of her habits. Oliver stayed with me and Kenn returned home. Mum had an x-ray and it initially confirmed that she had a fracture of her wrist but no injury to her hip. A plaster cast was put on her right arm. She was not at all amused by this. When the staff had seen to her she returned to The Grange and it seemed as if things would now go back to normal.

On Sunday, March 28, I received a phone call in the early morning hours from the nursing home. I was told that Mum had removed her plaster cast and that she would have to return to the hospital. When asked why she had removed the cast, Mum replied that she didn't have a fracture, so why should she have to put up with the cast on her arm—there was clearly no need! The staff assured me that they could get her to the hospital as I could not be there this time. We had our grandson, Lennon, staying with us and I didn't feel right waking the rest of the family at such an early hour. I told the member of staff that I would be at The Grange to visit Mum first thing.

An amazing thing—the nursing home staff rang me when Mum returned from the hospital. Apparently, she had been right! Another x-ray had confirmed that she did not have a fracture! Later, when I visited Mum and asked her why she had removed the cast, she told me that there was no way that she was meeting my father wearing that thing on her arm!

As Mum settled back in, we made preparations for her upcoming birthday celebration. The nursing home gave her a lovely party on the actual day. I managed to get there to film Mum as the rest of the family would not be able to visit until that evening.

We had a marvelous time and Mum was singing "Danny Boy" with all the other patients joining in. Mum also managed to record a message for all of her family. The message was one of love for all of her children, grandchildren, and great-grandchildren, and thankfulness for her wonderful son-in-law, my husband, Kenn.

For the first time Mum seemed to forget about going back to her home.

Most of the family came to visit Mum except Rose and Johnnie, who were both not feeling well. Mum seemed so very happy that we were there but she did realize that two of her children were missing. We had not reminded Mum that Charlie and his wife Anne had passed to spirit. Mum had been told when each passing had happened but because of her dementia she had forgotten.

~∽~

Mum received many cards and flowers for her birthday and as the celebration wound down, the commingled fragrances of those flowers filled the room. Mum became quieter and quieter as if the event, though joyful, had drained her of her limited energy.

I had noted earlier that her left leg was swollen and badly bruised and I began to feel on a deep level that there was something more ominous going on. I requested that a doctor look at the leg and he came in about two hours later and offered no new information. I was still deeply concerned, but there was little I could do and that helpless feeling swept through me

Saturday, April third came, and I went to the nursing home early as Mum was having her hair washed and set for her party. My niece, Catherine, was already there with her daughter, Siobhan. Mum seemed in good form and was looking forward to the evening. We got her dressed for the party in a lovely navy blue suit with a coordinating silk scarf around her neck. She also wore a pair of new black shoes. I commented to Mum that she looked very trendy in her Lycra tights and she gave me one of her precious smiles. I asked her if I could put a little makeup and lipstick on her and she agreed, since it was a special birthday.

As the time for the party approached I experienced a deep sense of both anticipation and trepidation as I again had the sensation of time slipping through my fingers, but I was determined to make this the best birthday party she had ever had.

Fergus arrived and we both accompanied Mum to the Lane Head Hotel in Brighouse where other family and friends were awaiting our arrival. Everyone was so happy to see Mum. I glanced at my brother Oliver and could see the sadness plainly visible on his face. Even though he was unaware of what had been shared with me in spirit from Dad and Harry, I felt that he somehow sensed things about Mum.

We took Mum around in her wheelchair to meet everyone and she was able to recognize most of the people present. When she realized that she was surrounded by only six of her nine children (as Johnny and Rose were missing) she never asked why they weren't there. She did meet and talk with my brother Charlie's children; again she never mentioned either the absence of Charlie or his wife Anne, whom she had loved dearly. I do believe that the reason she never asked after them is because she was, on some level, aware that they were in spirit.

As I looked around the room I could clearly see that it was not only full of those family and friends who were physically present, but also members of the family who had passed into spirit. Those who had passed had come to honor Mum on her birthday. At one point Mum reached out as if to greet someone who stood next to her chair. I could see clearly that it was Dad who was there beside her.

The party was in full swing and three of Mum's great-granddaughters did some Irish dancing and she really seemed to enjoy that. Her eldest grandson, Jim, gave a speech on behalf of all the grandchildren and great-grand-children and then I took over to thank everyone for coming and celebrating Mum's 90th birthday.

It wasn't until after the speeches were over that Mum seemed to fail a bit as if she were no longer a part of the festivities. We managed to have her cut her birthday cake, which was decorated in the Irish flag colors of green, white, and gold, and Mum said a few words with great difficulty. Once again, she sang along to one of her favorite songs, "Danny Boy."

There had been lots of joy and laughter shared for Mum's party but the underlying sense was one of sadness and tears held at bay. Just prior to leaving the party Mum had me take her around in her wheelchair so that she could say goodbye to everyone. Shortly afterward Fergus and I and Noreen, a friend of mine from Ireland, returned Mum back to The Grange where she was greeted by all the staff as if she were royalty.

Later, when I changed Mum into her nightclothes, I took notice of how frail and small she suddenly seemed, and I could hear Dad saying that she looked as slim today as she had the first day he met her. Dad urged me to go back to the party and enjoy the rest of the evening. Noreen looked at me, gave me a hug and without any words passing between us divined what I was thinking and feeling. Then she said, "I am so glad that I have made this journey to share in your mum's celebrations" and we both broke down and cried. Mum noticed that I was upset. She lifted her head and looked at me and said, "I have now completed everything that I wanted for you all and I want you to put a notice in the local newspaper thanking everyone for all their kind donations to the Alzheimer's Society instead of gifts." That was my mum, I thought—always concerned about helping everyone else.

Fergus, Noreen, and I returned to the party, and had a lovely evening singing and dancing and enjoying the rest of the celebration until around two in the morning.

Sunday morning, Kenn and I went to the nursing home as soon as we could. Mum looked in good form and wanted to know which friends had been to her party. We were able to tell her and to read all of the birthday cards she had received from family and friends. That was when she turned to me and said, "I haven't heard you read one out from Charlie and Anne." I hesitated and before I could come up with an answer she said, "Oh, why am I saying that when I know they have already gone?" Then I noticed that she kept looking up at the ceiling. I looked up as well, and who should I see above her head but Dad, Charlie, Anne, and John Joe, Charlie's twin brother who had passed when he was two days old.

Mum just seemed so happy.

It was as if she couldn't wait for her long sleep.

◯◠◯

The new week began.

My sister-in-law, Eileen, Peter's wife, thought it would be a good idea if we had a book in Mum's room so that all of us could leave a comment of how she was when they visited. Also, we would be able to read about any visitors she had had throughout the day. The book idea worked very well and it was heartening to read no concerns or comments about Mum's condition. Everyone seemed pleased with her obvious well-being when they visited.

On Monday, I visited Mum and she told me that the time was near for her to leave us and rejoin Dad, but she asked, "Is there not a birthday close?" I said that there was and that it was Johnnie's upcoming on April 13, which was the next day. She said, "I cannot go then, but I will go the day after." She looked up at me and gave me that smile that spoke volumes. She knew beyond a doubt who would be coming for her. I agreed with her that if she felt the time was right that it was only fair that we let her go.

I couldn't wait to get out of the room.

Mum kept looking up at me as if to say that she knew how sad I was.

Then she made a remark that took me by surprise. She said, "When your dad chose you to be called after me, I knew that my name would never die and that, somehow, the special child he longed for had come."

I couldn't answer her. I gave her a hug and left.

At 10:15 p.m. that night, I rang the nursing home just before I went to bed. I had a feeling that something had happened to Mum.

The nurse was very understanding and went straight to Mum's room to check to see if she was okay. Mum asked her who was on the telephone and the nurse told her it was me. Mum said, "I might have known it was Bridget," and it was left at that.

I lay awake all that night thinking about everything Mum had said to me that day and during the previous weeks.

The moments and seconds of that invisible clock were ticking away and I realized that the day I had never wanted to come was only twenty-four scant hours away.

∽

Wednesday, April 14 came, and from the moment I woke that morning the day seemed somehow tinged with a different feel, as if a myriad of emotions were colliding all around me.

I had to telephone the Ossett Spiritualist Church where I was to have taken the service that evening and tell them that I would, unfortunately, not be able to. They were a bit surprised that I had to cancel but when I explained to them that my mum was passing over in spirit and that I needed to spend as much time with her as I could, they understood and asked me if I would be able to take the service April 21, which I agreed to.

As soon as Kenn got home from work, I went straight to the nursing home.

The moment we got off the lift I could hear Mum shouting, "Take me home to Malham Road! Somebody please take me home!"

The sound of pathos in Mum's voice cut through my heart and I dreaded going into the room where she was; however, I had no choice.

As we entered I could clearly see that Mum was extremely distressed and seemed unaware of where she was. When she saw me she said, "Oh thank God you are here, Bridget!" I sat and held her hand and asked her what was wrong. She said, "Please take me home." It was a plea that hurt me terribly, but one I knew I was helpless to do anything about. I asked her why she wanted to go home and she told me that she needed to be in her own home today. During our conversation it became evident to me that Mum had been so distressed that she hadn't been able to get to the toilet quickly enough. I reassured her that after I had given her a shower I would seriously consider taking her home.

Peter and Billy arrived and saw how distressed Mum was. I asked them to please wait in Mum's room until a nurse and I had finished showering her. During the process I was shocked to see that her left leg was black from her hip to her toes and yet I was told that all the bruising was from her fall at home, which had been two weeks previous. And further that the severe bruising was caused because she was on aspirin. While I was showering her I could hear Dad saying, "At least it's you, Bridget, who's getting her ready for when that time comes." My feelings were careening nearly out of control and I tried hard to hold them at bay and get on with the task at hand. The experience of showering Mum took me back to my nursing days and I did my best to detach my emotions from what I was doing for my mother.

When her shower was done I found that, strangely enough, she had no clean nightgowns to wear as they were all in the wash. This was very hard to believe as she had had so many bought for her birthday. There was no choice but to dress her in a pink nightgown and dressing gown that belonged to the nursing home. This made me ask *why*? Had fate somehow intervened even down to the choice of clothing Mum was to wear for her last earthly hours?

When Mum was finally back in her room, she seemed to settle down and going home was never mentioned again. But she did sit and stare longingly out the window in the direction of Malham Road. I am sure that she realized that she would never be returning to her home again.

Kenn, Peter, and Billy were seated on Mum's bed. Billy smelled heavily of alcohol and seemed to be irritating Peter, who asked if I could take Billy home. By this time it was eight o'clock and Kenn and I were quite hungry, yet I didn't want to leave Mum. Kenn was all for us going to get something to eat and then returning to the nursing home.

I had a feeling deep inside that if I left I might not make it back in time to say goodbye to Mum, so I took advantage of the moments I had to say to her the things I needed to.

I got a chair and sat on it in front of her and took her hands in mine. "Mum," I said, "there is something I need to say to you." She looked at me and asked, "What is it, Bridget?"

I began to realize that this might possibly be the last time I spoke to Mum while she was still in physical form. I said, "Today's the day that is so different. Kenn and I are going to get something to eat and come straight back, but I want you to know that I love you with all my heart. I always have and I always will." She looked at me and said, "And I love you with all of my heart too, Bridget."

I turned to Billy and asked him to tell Mum how much he loved her. Of course, he wanted to know why I was asking this and I told him I would explain it later. He bent over her, gave her a kiss, and said, "I love you, Mum."

"Aah, Billy," was all she said.

After this she looked up at the ceiling and we all followed her gaze. I could plainly see Dad, Charlie, John Joe, and Anne gazing down at Mum and I knew deep in my heart that, no matter how much I begged them not to take her, the end was coming near.

Mum gave all of us a beautiful smile and said, "Be off with ya. I'll be fine, won't I?" as she looked up again at those gathered in spirit who still hovered near the ceiling.

Kenn, Billy, and I left. Peter decided to stay a bit longer with Mum.

Even though I was hoping to be back in time, I knew as I walked out the door of her room that I had said my last words of farewell to Mum.

We took Billy home. I did not go into the house with him. I told him that I would be ringing him later.

He didn't ask why.

Kenn and I went to the Waiters Arms Public House and I had the privilege of meeting Noleen and Martin, the land-lady and landlord of the establishment. Our conversation centered on talking about Mum. While there I ordered a Bulmer's cider and Kenn had a pint of Guinness. Kenn said to me, "You do know this is it, don't you, Bridget?" Then he continued. "When your mum looked up to the ceiling, I saw everything too."

We never did have anything to eat.

The entire time we were there I was fighting the incred-ible sense of urgency to return to the nursing home.

Time now seemed to speed up.

Suddenly, I experienced a very sharp pain in my chest.

I looked up at the clock. It was 10:15 p.m. and the first thought that crossed my mind was "Oh, God! I need to get to Mum now!" I knew something had happened.

Just at that moment my mobile phone rang. It was a withheld number and so I thought it must be our son, Marcus, ringing from home. I answered and said, "Hello, Marcus" only to hear a woman's voice. She asked me who she was speaking with and I told her. She said she was from my mother's nursing home. This would turn out to be Lesley, the manager of the nursing home.

I knew what she had called to tell me.

"It's Mum, isn't it?"

"Yes," she replied.

"She's gone, hasn't she?"

"Yes," she said. "I am so sorry to say so. At 10:15 p.m."

The precise time I had felt the pain in my chest.

Lesley informed me that no other family members had been notified so I requested that she not ring anyone else as I would contact them myself.

The events of my life now seemed to be happening around me—almost as if I were outside of my body looking in.

Noleen and Martin were very sympathetic but were at a loss for words. As we left the Waiters Arms and went home, my own thoughts were spiraling through the first stages of grieving—those thoughts and feelings that grasp at the heart as the mind begins to comprehend that a void has been created that can never be filled.

When we arrived home Marcus met us at the door. He seemed very scared and tried to relay information to me about an event that had happened in our home while he was alone there. I tried to listen to him, but being inconsolable I regretfully, for that moment, turned him aside. Marcus had telephoned my daughter Elizabeth with the news and she arrived to support Marcus. As I didn't know what Mum was going to look like, I didn't want the children to see her in a sad state, but rather felt it best that they hold on to their memories of her as a vital and alive human being.

For some reason, Kenn and I took a taxi to the nursing home. While on the way I decided to begin the process of telephoning the family and letting them know of Mum's passing. My first call was to Oliver. His girlfriend, Linda, answered and when I got Oliver on the phone I told him the news. It was as if he already knew.

I left it with Oliver to telephone Peter. I knew Peter's wife, Eileen, was probably away at work.

I phoned my eldest sister, Kathleen, gave her the news and then decided to cease calling for the time being. I felt that Rose, Johnnie, and Billy might not be able to accept that Mum had passed. Just as we were nearing the nursing home, my father spoke to me: "Ring Johnnie as they have a right to know." I did as Dad had instructed and Billy answered. I asked to speak with Johnnie. When I got my brother on the phone and told him he seemed very calm and I spent some moments reassuring him about Mum's wishes. When I asked him if he wanted to come to the nursing home to see Mum, he replied, "I didn't get to see her when she was alive so I think it is not fair to go now." And it was left at that.

There was a slight dilemma because my brother Fergus and his wife, Pam, had just gone to Spain on April 13. It was a consolation that I knew Fergus had been to visit Mum before he left. He told me afterward that he knew deep down that he would never speak to her again in this life. It was decided to wait to contact Fergus until April 15.

❧

When we arrived at the nursing home we were met by Lesley, the manager, who had telephoned me with the news. There were also two policemen and two paramedics present. It was explained that the policemen were present as Mum's death had been a sudden one. I was thinking then that Mum had chosen her time to pass and would these young men even understand me if I told them that. They were very sympathetic and, of course, they also had a job to do.

It was quite obvious that there had been an attempt to resuscitate Mum.

Mum was on her bed and lying in the opposite direction, still wearing the same pink nightgown and dressing gown that I had put on her earlier in the evening. She looked so very peaceful and as if she were just fast asleep. I leaned over and kissed her still-warm body. I noticed that her rings had been removed and placed on the dressing table, so I picked them up and slipped them onto the fingers of my right hand. I wanted to hold onto them until they were needed again; it was also comforting to physically be in contact with something she had worn.

Even though there were quite a few people in the room there seemed to be a vortex of calm surrounding Mum and the area near her. We were able to spend a few minutes with her and then Kathleen, her husband, John, their grandson Oliver, Oliver and Linda, Peter, myself and Kenn were taken into the sitting room and it was explained to us what had transpired.

Two nurses had gone into Mum's room around 10:00 p.m. to put Mum to bed and she was just finishing off her rosary. Mum asked the nurses if they would come back at 10:15. When they returned as she had requested they found that she had passed. It was as if she didn't want anyone to be upset at seeing her passing. I knew that she had not been totally alone during her transition to spirit as Dad, Charlie, John Joe, and Anne had been in the room when we arrived.

I was hurt and grieving but I was also peaceful and so glad that I had taken the opportunity to tell Mum how much I loved her.

An undertaker arrived and Mum's body was removed. Despite the fact that she was taken from the room with dignity, it still hurt to see her leave. We all stayed in the sitting room and tried to come to terms with our loss.

The police spoke to me and said that the coroner would be in touch at about nine the next morning as Mum's death was classified as sudden, and a postmortem would have to be carried out. This was something I had dreaded as I knew exactly what was involved because of my days in the nursing profession.

⌒⁄◯

We all left the nursing home and went our separate ways.

Peter took Kenn and me home and then he would go to Johnnie and Billy's. He would see Rose first thing in the morning. Elizabeth and Mathew had returned to their homes as well. Elizabeth hugged me and said that she knew that there was nothing anyone could say or do that could describe how everyone was feeling.

Kenn and Marcus were talking to me but I cannot recall all that they were saying. I know that it felt comforting to have them there but, at the same time, I had this overwhelming feeling that Marcus was thinking that I had lost my mum and what would he feel if he were in the same position.

Marcus was still very distressed and said to me, "Mum, can I just tell you what has happened tonight?" I listened closely as he told his story.

He went on to say that he had been sitting in the living room working on his computer when Benson, our black Labrador, started barking loudly and running back and forth between the dining room and the lounge. Marcus said he took his headphones off and when he did he could hear very loud music coming from the dining room. He got up and went into the room and found that our CD recorder was turned on and playing "Take Me Home to Mayo." He said aloud, "Okay, Grandma, I know it's just you, letting me know that you are safe."

I looked at my son. This, coupled with the events of the last days and hours, was both difficult and reassuring.

I went over to the CD recorder and took out the CD that was in it. Sure enough, this CD was a mixture of Irish songs and the track that it had stopped on was "Take Me Home to Mayo."

I knew that Mum, as Marcus had said, had wanted him and us to know that she was safe.

I pondered for a moment.

Mum had already chosen the songs she wanted played after she passed over, and even though "Take Me Home to Mayo" wasn't on the list, I felt in my heart that she wanted that song included, as well as "Edelweiss" (which I can only think was one of her choices because in the film *The Sound of Music* there were so many children to look after). The other song was "When You Were Sweet 16," a song that had been very special to Mum and Dad.

◦◦◦

Tying up the loose ends of a loved one's life for their memorial service is never easy.

On Thursday, April 15, I waited for the coroner to call at 9:00 a.m. When he rang he had a few questions for me to answer. He wanted to know if Mum's date of birth was correct. He told me the date he had and I confirmed that it was right. He remarked that Mum didn't look ninety, but rather looked more like seventy and I thought this to be a truly beautiful compliment.

When we got on the subject of the postmortem, he told me that it would be necessary as Mum hadn't been expected to die. Because Mum's body was to leave England to be buried in Ireland, it was very important that any foul play be ruled out. There could be no unanswered questions or concerns, such as her death being a result of the fall she had at the nursing home.

Two hours later he confirmed to me that Mum had died of natural causes which, in a way, was exactly as predicted. We would now be able to go ahead with our preparations to take Mum home to Ireland.

But before that could happen, Mother Nature was about to throw us a curve.

A volcanic eruption in Iceland caused a high-altitude cloud of ash to drift south and east, closing airports and cancelling all flights in northern Europe.

❦

We managed to contact Fergus in Spain and because of the situation with the ash cloud he was unable to fly back home.

It is a tradition in Ireland that the eldest son takes care of all the arrangements in connection with the funeral of a family member. With Charlie's passing, Fergus was now the eldest and we looked up to him.

Fergus received the news of Mum's passing with great dignity.

Throughout the entire ordeal of making certain that Mum's journey back to Ireland for burial was done in a manner she would have appreciated, I was in constant contact with Dad. He assured me that Mum had arrived safely as he had been the one to come and get her, along with Charlie, John Joe, and Anne. This made me feel very peaceful and I was grateful that all her wishes had been granted and that she was reunited with Dad and the others.

～⌒～

Taking Mum's body back to Ireland would not occur until April 28. This delay was actually a good thing as it allowed family to visit her at the funeral home as well as the hospital mortuary. During my visits to her, I came to terms with the fact that it was only the shell I was viewing and I found peace in the acceptance of her passing.

I was also able to choose an outfit for her to wear and to place her wedding ring back on her finger. I recalled that once I had asked Mum if I could have her wedding ring after she passed because I was named after her. She told me that the ring must stay on her finger just as Dad had placed it all those years ago, so that when they met again he would see it. "Till Death Us Do Part"—I quite liked her sense of humor.

∽

Two days after Mum passed over, and while her body was still in the funeral home, she returned in spirit to visit me.

She was with Dad and they both looked so happy to be back together again. I was quite amazed that she wasn't wearing the clothes that we had put on her for her burial but it was wonderful knowing that she had reached her destination. It was as if Mum had regained her youth, and she looked radiant.

I asked her if she could answer some questions for me and she said, "Yes."

My first question was, "Did you pass peacefully?"

"Yes I did, Bridget, with your dad, Charlie, Anne, and John Joe by my side."

"What did you feel, Mum?"

"I felt that I had instilled enough love within all of you for you to be able to carry on without me."

"Apart from Dad and the family coming for you, what was awaiting you when you got to heaven?" I asked.

"I was amazed first of all by the surroundings. It was just like I was going to a new home for the first time. Everyone, like my mum and dad, Harry, Great-aunt Bridget and my brother, your grandma and granddad off your dad's side, were all there to welcome me back home," she said.

"That's lovely, Mum," I said, feeling such joy and comfort in the conversation we were having. "What kind of place is heaven?"

"It's like home, but there is no pain or suffering. We leave that on earth but we do take memories from Earth to Heaven and my memories are lovely as I had the opportunity of meeting all of my children, grandchildren, and great-grandchildren."

My last question to Mum was, "Will you know when I need your help with anything?"

"Yes, I will, as I walk beside you always. It doesn't matter what time of day or night it is, I have learned that we can return to earth as and when needed, but there may be times when I am called to help someone else too."

"Oh, Mum," I said. "That surprises me. I thought that families just worked with families."

"No, there are people on earth who have no family, so we are called to support those whose need is the greatest."

"That's just typical of you, isn't it, Mum?" I said. "Do you remember when you used to wake all the neighbors up when we moved to Thornhill Road back in the '70s? They never needed an alarm clock as you were that clock so that they would all be up in time for work."

"I do," she said, with a lovely smile.

"Take a rest now, Mum. I feel you have won your crown."

We were to have two funerals for Mum—one in England and the other in her home place of Straide, County Mayo. The priest from her local church in Brighouse, where she had attended every Saturday evening up until a year before her passing, was less than kind and helpful. All our feelings were very hurt because we weren't allowed to play any of the songs Mum had requested—and this was done for reasons known only to the priest.

The church was packed for the first funeral in England and I gave the eulogy with great pride, telling people all about Mum's life from the very beginning to the very end. I ended it with the following poem I had written for Mum on behalf of all her family. This was actually given to me by Mum back in February of 1991 when she sat with me and listed, in order, each child born.

A TRIBUTE TO OUR MOTHER

Number one is Kathleen, she was our first child.
Your dad, he was overwhelmed and always by my side.
Number two was Charles, of course, he was a twin
My body was so swollen and then became so thin.
I lost Charles' brother but it was not in vain
Only six months later I'm pregnant again.
Number three was Fergus, the one I've waited for
Before I even realized, Johnnie was number four
Then along came Billy, he was number five
This time we were both so ill, in fact, he nearly died.
I took a little break as I needed a rest

Your dad, he took over, he really was the best.
Then along came Rose, she was number six
The biggest of my children, weighing eight pounds six.
Then, of course, came you, the apple of his eye
Not only number 7, you really made him cry.
He was very proud for daughter number three
And as you'll understand he named you after me.
Then along came Peter, child number eight
I really started to panic; we were running out of space
But how wrong could I be and for the very last time
"It's a boy," the nurse said, baby number nine.
We both named him Oliver; he was to be our last
My body was now tired and time was passing fast.
I'm very proud to own you all and you will always be
The one who was so special to both your dad and me.
Dad is now in heaven, I'll join him one day
But before I leave you, this is what I want to say:
Always be together in everything you do
And, as parents, we will always try to grant your wishes too.
It has been a pleasure to put this into verse
A tribute to our mother
We all feel truly blessed.

—Bridget Benson

We all watched as Johnnie helped to carry Mum's coffin out of the church to the waiting hearse so that it could be taken to the airport for the flight back to Ireland the next day. Sadly, Johnnie and Rose would not be able to attend the funeral in Ireland.

Mum's mass was followed by a reception at the church hall for those people who would not be able to travel to Ireland. This was the first time all of Mum's family and friends had been together without her physical presence, but to me she was right there, walking among all of us and making herself known by flashing lights and the lovely smell of roses that trailed along with her.

After the reception ended, we all returned to our homes in preparation for meeting at the airport for the trip to Ireland for Mum's funeral and burial.

I kept thinking that everything would be fine as now Mum's body was on the first part of her journey back home to Ireland. Her body was taken care of by the officials at Manchester Airport overnight and we would be joining her the next day, April 29, when we all would travel to Ireland together. At check-in the airport staff were very helpful and supportive. Even the cabin crew onboard the airplane seemed to know why we were all traveling together, although we never said anything to them.

While we were onboard the airplane, Mum began to speak to me from spirit. She wanted to tell me that she wasn't the only one in cargo. There was a gentleman whose body was also being returned to Ireland for burial. She said that she was having a good conversation with him.

"What are you like, Mum?" I asked.

"You don't think that I am staying quiet for this one-hour journey, do you?" she replied.

I started laughing and thought that it was a shame that no one else could hear our conversation, although my family did look at me a bit strangely—as if I were going crazy.

When we arrived at Knock Airport, we had to wait two hours for clearance so that we could get Mum's body to the church. The coffin was met by the second undertaker whom she had chosen years before to take her funeral when the time came. Mum obviously had foreseen what the future held—otherwise, I thought, how could she have known this man would be alive to carry out her wishes?

When her coffin came through, there were lots of people from Mum's village to welcome her back home. We were all very emotional and at the same time felt honored that so many people would make time for Mum as she had not lived in Ireland for forty-two years. These people followed the cortege for four miles or so to Straide Church. When we arrived at the church it was full, and again I paused and thought that even though Mum had left her birthplace years ago, we were surrounded by so many supportive people.

Mum's coffin was carried by Fergus, Peter, Oliver, and her three grandsons: Mathew, Mark, and Marcus. I looked at them and thought how proud Mum would be as they were all dressed in morning suits and looked top notch! I could hear whispers from people saying what a lovely family Mrs. O'Malley had. There were comments about how differently the bearers were dressed and many wondered who they were. I felt very honored that my two sons were old enough to carry Mum's coffin.

The aroma of red roses perfumed the hearse and the flowers also festooned the top of Mum's coffin. We were met by a young priest called Father Davey and I can honestly say that he made up for our disappointment at Mum's mass in Yorkshire. Although Father Davey had never met Mum, he gave a beautiful and dignified service.

The family was seated at the front of the church on the left-hand side and after the short service ended, suddenly people came forward to pay their respects. It took me back to when Dad died and I started reliving those memories all over again.

We didn't leave the church for nearly two hours as people were coming over constantly to speak with us. Some of them shared their memories and tales of Mum and how they respected the fact that even though Mum had been a young widow, she had never remarried and lived her life for her children.

After the church service, the family went to the Copper Beech public house where we were greeted by the owner, Brendan Maloney, who went over and above the call of duty to make sure that we were fed and looked after, which again made us feel very proud of Mum and the people and the place where we were born and brought up. Neighbors came forward to offer places for the family to stay, if needed, but we had already organized this. Everyone was so kind and Dad's name was mentioned many times.

People asked me how I felt being able to contact the spirit world. It was as if everyone wanted reassurance that this other world did exist. After I had spoken with most of them, I felt that they were comforted by what I had told them of my experiences.

We left the Copper Beech at a reasonable time to prepare ourselves for the next day.

Mum's mass would be at eleven o'clock and her burial would follow.

⌍⌎

Friday morning came.

Everyone looked extremely smart in their new shirts and ties. This time we had to sit on the right-hand side of the church. Again, the church was full of people turning out to support the family.

Marian Walsh sang "Edelweiss" and Frances McHale sang "Sweet Sixteen." "How Great Thou Art" and "Take Me Home to Mayo" were also sung by Frances McHale when Mum's body left the church.

When we came out of the church, the rain was coming down heavily. I remembered Mum always saying, "Blessed is the soul that the rain falls on." I thought that she had gotten her wish.

I was concerned that this time the coffin had to be carried a long way to Mum's grave, which was already prepared next to Dad's, but Mum's three sons and three grandsons managed to lower the coffin into the grave as this is the usual tradition.

I could hear cries and sobs in the background yet there were no tears in my eyes as I knew it was just Mum's shell in the coffin. I looked up. There above us, looking down, were Mum, Dad, and my brothers and sister-in-law.

We all threw a rose on top of Mum's coffin and then left to go back to the Copper Beech for Mum's reception, which, I have to say, was fantastic. The caterers and Brendan did us proud.

It was lovely to see that most people were able to join us in what was to be our final farewell to Mum.

Most of the family returned to England that Saturday but myself, Kenn, Fergus, and Billy stayed until Monday, May 3, just to check that the grave was filled in and to visit Mum's remaining relatives. It was nice hearing stories about Mum; most of those stories were about when Dad passed and Mum had to make life-changing decisions about leaving Ireland.

During the extra time spent in Ireland, I learned so much about Dad—heartwarming tales of how Dad had always done the weekly shopping and how the donkey and cart were always full of groceries. I was told how Dad always had food on the table, even when times were bad all over

Ireland with work or if we hadn't produced full crops for the year.

It was when I was visiting the home of my cousin, Mary Knight, that I decided to go back to the house where I was born. When I arrived I went to sit on the wall outside and I could see all the leprechauns, fairies, and spirit children that I had played with as a child. The child spirits were now adults. And to my surprise, dancing in the middle of the ring of those wonderful beings there were Mum and Dad! The tears were streaming down my face, but I can't say that they were tears of sadness. It was just so emotional for me seeing Mum and Dad together again. They looked so very happy. They asked me why I was upset. I tried to explain that for the first time the reality had finally hit me that they were in another world and, although I, above all, understood this, the pain was still so raw.

I stayed at the house for at least twenty more minutes and was able to finally put closure on the home, but not the memories.

❧

I rejoined my family for a couple more hours and then we returned home, where we met with some friends and continued our Irish wake. A wake entails talking and remembering the people who have passed. There is also celebration with food and alcohol. Mum's wake went on until late that night.

On Monday, May 3, we returned to England.

It was the day before Fergus's birthday. We mentioned it and wondered if Mum would remember his birthday. We didn't have to wait long before a message came.

"Of course I know it is Fergus's birthday on Tuesday, and I wish him well as he has always been so good to me," Mum said from spirit.

I passed the message on to Fergus but he just looked at me and said nothing. I could sense that he was sad because, even though he had visited Mum before he had left for Spain, he had never actually gotten the opportunity to say a real goodbye. He was proud, however, that he had carried out all of Mum's final wishes.

On the return trip, it seemed strange that there were only four of us going home instead of the nearly twelve that had originally gone to Ireland. As I sat on the plane my thoughts turned again and again to the funeral, to Mum and Dad being together once more—their bodies in the grave together. On one level I knew that it was only their shells that were there, but it was still very difficult to accept it. It was also difficult trying to explain to Billy that it was only Mum's shell that we had buried and not her soul. Her soul was in heaven.

I did my best to try to imagine how Billy felt, but the unmistakable pain on his face said it all. The long days of around-the-clock care he had given Mum before she had gone to The Grange were over. Everyone was very quiet and I could clearly sense that he was thinking about this perhaps being his last journey to Ireland. I assured him that we would visit Ireland and the grave as often as we could and this we have continued to do to this day.

When we arrived at Manchester Airport, Fergus and Billy left together in their car and Kenn and I made ready to leave in ours. Despite the fact that the terminal was very busy, it was as if a deep silence had descended over the place.

I closed my eyes just for a bit to capture the scene and then, on the way home, I fell asleep.

❧

Tuesday came and we all wished Fergus a happy birthday.

I was working and I wondered how I was going to feel during the appointments, especially if I found that someone had recently lost their mum. However, when I looked in the diary, I saw that all the appointments had been in touch offering their condolences and to rearrange, just to give me that little bit of extra time.

Our grandson Lennon's second birthday was on Thursday, May 6, and we had a very nice time. It was interesting that in the middle of our family get-together Lennon mentioned that Great-Grandma was in Heaven. He then gave me a big hug and it was as if he knew what had been going on.

Each day after Mum's burial was different. Some days I coped very well, as if nothing had ever happened, and then other days I was totally consumed with Mum's loss.

I returned to Ireland on May 13 especially for Mum's Month's Mind Mass, a tradition in Ireland that is done to remember the first month of a loved one's passing. Once again, familiar faces filled the church. After the mass, I began to feel more and more like I could move on.

For the two weeks that I was in Ireland, I was busy with appointments. It was so very comforting to feel that Mum, Dad, and I were together in Ireland and I managed to visit the grave without feeling that pain any more. In fact, it was as if I were visiting someone else's grave. When I got to the graves, there was one thing that made me smile—all the flowers were being finished off by three baby rabbits. I could hear Mum saying, "Well, they do need feeding. I don't mind."

I turned to walk away from the grave and paused. The lovely view from Mum and Dad's graves across the valley caught my eye. I thought what a beautiful place Mum had chosen over forty years ago to be her final resting place.

⌒✿⌒

In the aftermath of the funerals and Mum's burial, I had a chance to reflect on my own feelings about her passing. I knew I had delayed my grieving as I had tried to be strong for everyone else, especially Johnnie and Billy, who had shared so much with Mum. I had also done my best to reassure Marcus, who had been extremely close to his grandma, that she had looked very peaceful and as if she just were asleep after she passed. It was very important to me that he remember only the happy moments he had shared with his grandmother and that now, after a long life, she was with Granddad, whom she had so longed to be reunited with for many years.

I wondered if I had done everything that had been expected of me. Even though I had two sisters who were older than me, I felt that Mum would turn to me when times were difficult. Perhaps I felt this extra burden because I was called after my mum and so had the responsibility to be that loving, caring daughter who wouldn't be here without all the sacrifices Mum had made for me.

I also wondered if I should have taken her back home for her last night. I could hear Dad reassuring me that it was best that she didn't pass over in her home for the sake of Johnnie and Billy's feelings. And so my worries vanished in the comfort of my father's reassurance.

I spent some time allowing my thoughts to turn back to my childhood and all the good and not-so good times. Then I became aware of what Mum must have gone through during her final days here on earth. I know she was so happy to be joining again with Dad, but I am sure she had intense feelings of remorse for leaving us all behind—especially Billy, whom she had protected all his life, and who now, like the rest of us, had to cope.

Both Mum and Dad visited me with such love that I knew would last forever and this was so comforting. After their visits, they would vanish into what appeared to me to be a magical vapor.

A huge sense of peace came over me and at last I felt as if all my worries and all my questions had been answered.

Mum would never be far away from me and I knew in my heart that she had earned her crown.

CHAPTER 2
Shadow and Light

Every day our lives are filled with a blend of both shadow and light—good and joyful events often have as a precursor some shadow moments that allow us, in the end, to find the beauty in the extraordinary days of light and contentment.

So it was not long after Mum's passing I knew I was going to face the loss of my brother, Johnnie.

I recall that it was after our brother Charles's funeral in January of 2009 that Johnnie had told me that he had cancer and was going to be the next to pass to spirit. When he told me this I looked at him in astonishment, but at the same time my gut feeling was that he was telling the truth.

Johnnie had been passing blood from his back passage. I listened to what he had to say and then asked him if he had been to his doctor. He told me that he had and that without examining him the doctor had given the diagnosis of hemorrhoids. I requested that Johnnie allow me to get him an appointment with a specialist and he agreed.

After the specialist examined Johnnie about a week later, he told him that there was a massive growth in his rectum and that they would need to do blood and other tests. When the results came back just a few weeks later, it was confirmed that Johnnie's growth was malignant. Because this growth was so high up in the rectum and bowel, the only surgery available was a colostomy.

I felt so very sad for Johnnie because he went on his own to see the consultant for the test results and for him to have been given this news with no one there for him must have been very difficult. But Johnnie told me that he was relieved about getting the results and knowing that he wasn't imagining anything was a comfort.

Johnnie was a very hard-working man and although he liked alcohol, he was the kindest man you would ever want to meet. He had lived with Mum and Billy for thirty-three years.

I recall that I had dreaded having to tell Mum that she was going to be losing another son. Mum adored Johnnie, probably because he so closely resembled our dad. Johnnie had requested that we keep the news from Mum and this was done, although it wasn't easy. Johnnie required twenty-eight weeks of chemotherapy and radiotherapy prior to the surgery. Through it all Johnnie was so brave and never once complained or asked, "why me?"

It wasn't until Johnnie had his surgery in October of 2009 that he at last gave me permission to tell Mum. When she got the news she was very sad and said, "Please tell me that I am not going to lose him." I told her the truth—that Johnnie might make a recovery but that there was also the chance that the cancer might return.

I still believe to this day that this is why our mum chose to make her arrangements for her own journey home as she couldn't bear to lose another member of the family.

And there was always the thought in my mind that the news of Johnnie's illness hastened Mum's own passing.

After Mum's passing, Johnnie talked a lot about how he would be so happy when the day came for him to join her and he even told me what songs he wanted played at his funeral. These were: "Candle in the Wind" by Elton John and "This World is Not My Home" by Jim Reeves. I asked my brother what the song "Candle in the Wind" meant to him and he told me to listen to the words. He said he felt like he was the candle in the wind who never knew who to turn to when the rain came in. He said that to the outside world he always seemed happy but inside no one knew him. In Johnnie's own words: "You will all understand why I want to go home" because there is a verse in the song "This World is Not My Home" about having a loving mother and how he couldn't wait until he shook her hand.

Johnnie went on to live his life to the fullest as best as he could. He saw more of his children and the family became one again despite many past differences.

On May 20, 2012, Johnnie was admitted to the hospital.

In the early morning hours of that day, Mum came to the side of my bed and gently woke me up to tell me that she had come to take Johnnie home and that she would be doing this tomorrow. I asked her why and she said, "He has had enough now, Bridget."

"Okay, Mum, but I haven't heard anything. Why hasn't anyone telephoned me?"

"Because no one knows yet, but your phone call will come later in the morning."

Sure enough, at 7:20 a.m. the phone rang and it was my sister Kathleen. She told me that Johnnie was very ill and that Billy was waiting for an ambulance.

Johnnie was transferred from the hospital to an infirmary where tests were carried out and he was diagnosed with obstruction of the bowel. A drip was put into his arm for the fluids he needed as it had been noticed that neither the catheter nor colostomy bag had been working properly.

These investigations went on all through Sunday and I decided to wait until Monday morning to go see what was happening as it had been mentioned that Johnnie could be taken to surgery. I kept in close contact with the family but as everyone seemed to have different stories I turned to Mum and Dad. Mum told me that it was important that I be with Johnnie when he passed over, so I went ahead and cancelled and rescheduled all of my appointments for Monday. After this, I went with Kenn and Billy to the infirmary.

Johnnie had never married and when we arrived we found that two of Johnnie's three children from a previous relationship were there with their mother. It was plain to see that even though Johnnie was in a great deal of pain he was able to hold a good conversation and he knew who we all were.

During the visit Billy became very upset after about an hour or so with his brother and he could not stay. Johnnie noticed that Billy was crying and asked him why he was doing that. Billy told his brother that he hadn't ever seen Johnnie looking like he did at that moment. Soothing Billy, Johnnie told him not to worry because he would be home soon. I thought he was referring to his home on earth and not his spirit home and that he was doing this to calm Billy. Very soon after this Kenn took Billy home.

I was now left in the room with Johnnie and his family. Johnnie kept looking at his son Paul. He finally said, "Well, Paul, I haven't seen you in a long time and today it is probably hello and goodbye."

Paul's sister Sharon told her father that she thought he would be okay and Johnnie just looked at her.

The nurse in me leapt to the fore when I noticed with some alarm that the fluid in the drip was pouring out onto the bed and that my brother would soon be lying on wet bedding. However, and more importantly, Johnnie would not be benefitting from the fluids. I left to have a word with the nurses and the doctor. Shortly afterward a nurse came in and removed Johnnie's drip; he was given pain medication and he seemed to settle down after this. His bedclothes were also changed.

I was to speak to the doctor regarding Johnnie's condition and whether further surgery would be needed, but the discussion didn't happen when it should have as the doctor was very busy on the ward. I had already explained to the staff that I had been a nurse. After this I began to feel very frustrated and sought out the nurse to tell her what I felt—that a patient leaving this world was as important as any other patient and should be treated with dignity and respect.

Throughout this entire time with my brother during his final hours, I had quietly been begging Mum and Dad to come and take him so that he would be free from his pain. It hurt me so terribly to see him in such agony—this dear man that our mum had called "our blue-eyed boy" as he so much resembled our dad.

Johnnie's family left, promising to return the next day. I stayed with him and we continued to talk about his passing and the fact that the last rites of the Catholic Church would be administered. I also asked Johnnie if there was anything that he wanted to talk to me about and he requested that since he didn't feel he was going to pass over just yet could we hold off on the priest coming. I let the question go unanswered and concentrated on talking with my brother about other, happier memories. As I sat there beside him,

I thought that even though it would have been nice to have other family members with us, I was actually very grateful to be alone with my brother and sharing his last moments with him.

I told Johnnie how much he meant to me and we spent some time reminiscing about so many good times such as him giving me away at my wedding in 1976. I remarked to him—as I had so many times before—how very much he looked like our dad. There were so many things I wanted to say to him—so many things that had seemed trivial but that now seemed, in the face of his imminent transition, to take on new meaning and urgency. I felt a great need to apologize to him for all the times I had argued with him about his drinking and told him I had only done it because I loved him so much. Thankfully he seemed to understand.

We also veered off onto the topic of his children and how he felt about them. This was a topic we had never really spoken of and as far as I knew no one in the family truly understood his feelings about the subject. He simply said that he loved them dearly and that he was a very private person. I did not discuss this any further as I felt he did not wish to talk about it. His children were grown up and one of his daughters had two sons. Sadly, none of them ever seemed to be a part of our family.

Shortly after this conversation the doctor arrived and asked to have a word with me. She was a young woman and very sympathetic and I know it must have been hard for her to deliver the news that Johnnie had less than an hour to live. She told me it was time to get the family in.

A great feeling of helplessness came over me but I had to put that aside. I telephoned the priest to come and I also phoned as many of the family as I could and included Johnnie's children who lived a distance away. When I got in touch with them they were shocked by what I was telling them. I left it that they would try to make it back in time.

When I got back to Johnnie's room, I could hear him speaking but as he did I felt as if the room were filling up with more people in spirit. He would open and close his eyes and began reaching out. Suddenly, he said, "Bridget, can you open that door?" As I moved closer to the wall, I saw two solid oak doors appear.

I asked Johnnie whom I would be opening the doors to and he said, "Mum and Dad."

As soon as he spoke, the doors simply opened up of their own accord and in walked our mum and dad, arm in arm. Although Mum had only passed over two years ago, she now appeared before us looking perfect and young. I looked at Dad and then back at Johnnie. It was amazing because the two men looked like twins. I could see that behind Mum and Dad were Charlie and his wife, Anne, and Charlie's twin brother, John Joe, followed by Mum's parents and lots of others I did not recognize.

At the sight of his family, Johnnie's face lit up with a beautiful smile. He reached out his arms to welcome Mum and Dad, and I could clearly see that he was overjoyed with what was awaiting him. He then spoke the name Kevil, saying, "Martin Kevil, fancy seeing you! I haven't seen you for such a long time!" I knew that Martin Kevil, who had been a good friend of Johnnie's in Ireland, had passed over at least nine years before from a heart attack.

This next occurrence was like a film unfolding on the screen in front of me, but it was much more real and magical.

Dad reached out to me as I reached out to him. Mum was holding Johnnie's hand and Dad held Mum's hand and I held Johnnie's other hand. The feeling of holding hands with Dad was so *real*—it was like I was holding hands with someone in physical form yet there was also a distinct tingling sensation much like a low electric shock going through my fingers. It was not at all uncomfortable; in fact, it was such a joyful thing to be able to touch my parents once again, even if it were only for a brief moment.

The circle of love around Johnnie was now complete.

The priest arrived shortly after and gave Johnnie the last rites. Before he left he remarked how young Johnnie looked.

After the rites were given, it was as if Johnnie felt he was free to go with Mum and Dad and the rest of the family back *home*.

I could feel now that it was time to let Johnnie go and I put my arms around him and mentioned all of his brothers' and sisters' names. I told him that we were going to really miss him and that he was in very safe hands with his family that had gone before him. Then I asked him if he would let me know when he had arrived safely. I closed my eyes and when I opened them I could see Johnnie standing between Mum and Dad and everyone else nearby. Just at that moment Fergus and Peter came into the room and Johnnie took his last breath. Soon afterward Kathleen arrived with her daughter, Mary. Oliver also got there but sadly, Johnnie's children did not make it.

Our brother Johnnie passed to spirit at 5:25 p.m. on Monday, May 21, just as Mum had said.

I stood looking down at the shell that my brother had left behind and I could see that all his pain and suffering had come to an end. Our brother Fergus was very emotional as we were left alone in the room to say our goodbyes.

Kenn came into the room and was shocked that Johnnie had passed over so quickly. Charlie's daughter Joanne and her partner John also came and I could see by the look on Joanne's face that she was reliving the passing of her own father three years earlier.

We stayed with Johnnie as long as we could and then took our leave. On the way out, Peter, who had been appointed by Johnnie as his executor, asked me if I could get in touch with the funeral director and this I did. It was to be the same place that had handled Mum's funeral and I knew that everything would be done in a caring and dignified manner.

In the midst of all the arrangements for Johnnie, I had an overwhelming feeling come over me that it was not the cancer that had taken my brother but rather something else—something had perhaps poisoned him, but as I had no proof I kept these thoughts to myself. If anything were meant to be revealed it would come to light.

It happened that I had to go pick up the death certificate, but when I telephoned I was told it was not ready as the cause of death was now being questioned. There was now talk about the feasibility of conducting an autopsy. Every part of me was on full alert—was this the way in which the real cause of my brother's death would be revealed?

Later, when I went with my friend, Linda, to pick up the death certificate at the registrar's office, I commented to the registrar that I couldn't understand why they were questioning the cause of death and wanted to do an autopsy. I was told that it was because Johnnie did not die of cancer—he died of sepsis due to a urinary tract infection that had been missed. The infection had eventually led to his major organs failing.

I was deeply hurt and disillusioned because Johnnie had had a catheter in that had not been checked in a week! While this was now validation of my instincts about the real cause of Johnnie's passing, it was, nonetheless, a horrible thing to find out and it brought every bit of my training as a nurse to the fore.

Before I left, the registrar asked me if the family wanted to go ahead with the autopsy. I looked at her and said from my heart, "I feel that he has suffered enough pain and the family will find it difficult to cope with an autopsy."

The woman was thankfully extremely understanding and went on to tell me that she had family members who were Irish. She issued the death certificate and Linda and I left.

After this episode in the registrar's office, the grieving finally hit me with mixed feelings of both peace and guilt. I thought that part of this was because I never really and truly grieved for Charles or Anne, but then when Mum passed I felt at peace because I knew she had gotten her wish to be back together with my father. Then again, maybe I was having all of these confusing feelings because of all the passings in my life coming so close together.

I went out to buy some clothes for Johnnie because I wanted him to look his best. He had new trousers in his wardrobe so it was a simple matter of getting a shirt, tie, and socks. I took all his things to the Chapel of Rest for them to dress him in. After this I decided to visit Johnnie at the funeral home. It would be a while before all the family and friends who were coming for the service could arrange their busy lives to attend. The service was scheduled for May 29 and 30.

When I saw Johnnie's body, I was a bit shocked as it did not look at all like the peaceful man I had seen pass over. There was great darkening of the skin caused by the sepsis so I had to explain to the undertaker that I didn't want his children seeing their father looking this way, especially Johnnie's daughter, who lived in Spain. The matter was soon nicely taken care of and when I next viewed my brother's body on the 28th he looked much more presentable.

Johnnie was removed to St. Joseph's Roman Catholic Church, Brighouse, and the cortege came past the house on Malham Road where he had lived with Mum and Billy for so many years. It was a reminder once again of the trip we had taken with Mum in April of 2010. This was a journey I had vowed not to take again, but here I was.

We arrived at the church to be met by so many of Johnnie's friends who welcomed and sympathized with all the family. Many of Johnnie's friends were crying and it made me feel so touched by the fact that my brother had been loved by so many people.

The coffin was carried into the church by Johnnie's nephews and our two younger brothers, Peter and Oliver. Johnnie would lay at rest in the church overnight.

At the funeral service and after the priest had said his prayers we sat and listened to the song "Candle in the Wind" by Elton John. Johnnie had favored a particular line in the song as it resonated to his feelings about no one really knowing him.

I wondered if this feeling of not being truly *known* had been one of the reasons Johnnie had so often turned to alcohol and spent such a lot of his time in his bedroom. It seemed to me that my brother had everything he could have wished for in his family—especially his brothers and sisters—and yet, I was feeling the deepest hurt because he had thought he was so alone. He had adored our mum and she him. Why had he never married when he had such a beautiful example in our parents?

Of course many of these questions would remain unanswered.

After the church service ended we all went our separate ways. Some went out for drinks but I went home to prepare myself for the next day which would be the burial. I just needed to be alone in the silence to think about the events of the week and try to come to peace with it all.

I went to bed and fell asleep. Almost immediately I began to dream. In the dream were Mum, Dad, Charlie, John Joe, Anne, Johnnie, and many others who appeared to be celebrating Johnnie's homecoming. Mum was serving dinner. When I looked at Johnnie, it was as if he had never been ill at all. I didn't want to come out of that dream, but when I woke up the impact of the dream hit me with the reality that Johnnie was truly gone from this earth.

Wednesday morning came and we all got dressed in our mourning outfits. Everyone looked very smart and we set off for the church as mass was to be at 10:30 a.m. The church was packed when we arrived. It was nice to see that so many had turned out for Johnnie and for us as a family. This was especially nice as this was a weekday and many people had traveled from all over the country to pay their respects. We also had family who had come in from Ireland.

The service was lovely. I did the eulogy and felt the presence of loved ones who had passed. I could hear Mum and Dad say, "You have done us real proud."

When the service concluded, we all stood and listened to Johnnie's final chosen song, "This World is Not My Home" by Jim Reeves. The words fit everything we knew to be true about Johnnie.

The coffin was now carried by family as we made our way to the graveyard at Smith House Lane, Brighouse. The spot was chosen for Johnnie as it was his wish to be buried in England and this had been discussed with his children. There were so many people at the graveyard but I felt that I was on the outside looking in and that I wasn't really there at all. I could hear people talking about Johnnie and what a fine man he was and that he was going to be so dearly missed.

After the burial we had two celebrations at two different venues. The main one was at the Lane Head Hotel and the other was at the Black Swan with both of these places being in Brighouse.

The Black Bull that Johnnie used to frequent was shut down and this gave all Johnnie's close drinking friends the opportunity to meet and remember all the good times they had had with Johnnie. Food was laid out at both establishments and as things progressed it didn't seem to me to be a sad event at all. In fact the day felt as if it were a celebration of Johnnie being taken from his pain and suffering and returning home with his family.

Thursday I was back at the office continuing with my work and the writing of this book. I could sense that Johnnie was with me as I recounted the memories of the last week or so, and even though my brother had left earth—the second brother in only three years—I came to greater peace with it. There are still seven of us remaining and I take great comfort in the knowledge that I will always be able to communicate with Johnnie and the rest of the family who have already passed to spirit.

About a month after his passing, Johnnie was in more direct contact with me, which gave Mum and Dad a much-needed rest.

I will never, ever forget the last words Johnnie spoke to me before he left with Mum and Dad: "We will meet again, Bridget."

Those words will remain with me until I am once again reunited with Johnnie and all my family, where I will also experience eternal peace.

Billy Moves on With His Life

After my mum and my brother Johnnie passed to spirit, a decision had to be made regarding Billy's welfare. He was now living alone in the home he had shared with the two of them for thirty-five years and it was felt that there were far too many memories in the house for him to cope with.

In order to get Billy a one-bedroom apartment, he had to fit the criteria required by the local authority. The house he was residing in was a three-bedroom semi-detached, owned by the local authority—and three-bedroom homes were in short supply.

I got in touch with Billy's doctor and had a meeting with her and Billy. She felt that it would be in Billy's best interest to move as soon as possible. She also thought that there were some vacant apartments close to the office where they could keep a close eye on Billy should it be needed.

I went through the appropriate channels and Billy was moved into a one-bedroom apartment near the doctor's office in July of 2012. The process of moving him was a harrowing one. Some family members went to Malham Road to help Billy pack up what was important to him. Each one of us removed special things that Mum had collected—things that Mum had acquired and many items we had given her over the years such as photographs of the children from birth onward, and many keepsakes that meant a great deal to us.

I found that sorting through these precious items was even harder for me to deal with than when Mum and Johnnie had passed because this process made it real. We were saying a final goodbye to all the memories we had shared in the home.

It was like leaving Ireland all over again.

Kenn and I also went to the house to collect other items that belonged to us and we spent two hours in Mum's bedroom just sitting on the bed, recalling all the conversations we had had over the years with her. Each photograph I picked up told a story. I even found newspaper clippings with articles about Christmas festivities and other special occasions they were all involved in. When I went through

Mum's jewelry, I only took the pieces that I had bought for her over the years.

When I was done I sat on the bed and looked around the room. All of Mum's blessed statutes and pictures were still on the walls. I cried until I didn't have another tear left to shed. Then I went from Mum's room into Johnnie's and I sat on his bed. Again I was overwhelmed with emotion and yet I could hear him saying, "Don't cry, Bridget. You always did the best for both Mum and me and like I told you on the day that I was passing over to spirit, we will meet again."

Despite Johnnie's words of comfort to me, the pain I was feeling was indescribable and a pain I did not want to feel again for a very, very long time.

I went downstairs and both Billy and Kenn could see that I had been crying, but there was silence and I knew they understood.

As I was walking through the lounge I looked at the unit (cabinet) that Johnnie had bought for Mum maybe three or four years before, which she had really loved. I heard her say, "You take that, Bridget, for your home, if it's alright with Billy as I know you will take care of it for me." I told Billy what Mum had said to me from spirit. I remembered too that, a while before Mum had passed, she had wondered where the unit would go after she was gone. Now she had made the decision that it was to be mine.

I pondered over how Kenn would feel as it was a big unit and when I asked him he said, "If your mum has said that, that is how it has to be."

The unit sits very comfortably in my dining room and although it is a bit old-fashioned, I have come to love it and I will treasure it always because a part of Mum's home is now in mine.

Johnnie spoke to me from spirit and asked, "Why don't you have my comfy chair from my bedroom for your office?"

Again, with Billy's permission, I now have that very comfortable chair in my office.

It is such a nice feeling to be surrounded by these things my mum and brother once cared for and it helps me to feel close to them and as if I really haven't lost them.

It was unfortunate that while Mum and Johnnie were alive Billy became a full-time caregiver—first to Mum and then to Johnnie in his later months. Billy never had time to think about himself or even to have a day off as it was a 24/7 job. Now everything has stopped and Billy has become ill. The weight has fallen off him and he is undergoing major tests on his bowels. These tests are still ongoing as each examination turns over a new problem.

We are all very proud of Billy. Even though there are times when he says things that can be very hurtful, we have to remember that although we have lost our mum and brother, a big part of Billy's life has now become empty. Most of the family are sympathetic but, as with most families, there is one here and there that has become distant to him. But, I know in my heart that I will always be there for Billy. And, as it has been for the past thirty-five years, he will be spending Christmas with us because that is a promise I made to

Mum and it will continue for as long as we are both here on earth.

Really and truly, I know I was born, as we all are, for a reason and caring for others and being there is what I have always done. Fergus, Peter, and Oliver have been hands-on in helping Billy and even though now, this Christmas, will be Billy's first without Johnnie, I am sure that both Mum and Johnnie will come to pay us a visit.

I have spoken with Billy on several occasions and reassured him that whatever happened in the past regarding decisions that had to be made by Mum's doctor that she be placed in The Grange were the very best for her at the time. Billy was also reassured that he had done the very best he could with caring for both Mum and Johnnie, and that he could have done no more. He is still very emotional and even though he is surrounded by all his personal possessions from Malham Road, I know that if he could he would do anything to turn back the hands of time.

Mathew and Rachel's Wedding

The light came back into our lives when our eldest son, Mathew, married Rachel on October 6, 2012 in Grasmere, which is in the Lake District, an area of great natural beauty with not only lakes, but also forests and mountains. Grasmere means a great deal to both Rachel's family and to Mathew as they have taken many vacations there since they first met seven years ago.

Just prior to the start of the ceremony I sent out my thoughts to those in spirit of both families and invited them to the wedding. Almost immediately Mum came and said, "Of course we are all going to be present and we will make sure that you know about it."

Mum's reassurance of the family's being present gave me great peace and comfort.

We all left as a family on October 4, as we were going to join Rachel and her bridesmaids for high tea. When we returned to the hotel that night, Mum came to me and said, "All the ladies are here." I could feel the presence of a great many people in spirit. My very intuitive mother-in-law, Penny, turned to me and said, "They have all come, haven't they, because I feel squashed on this bench."

Gathering around us in spirit were Jackie, Betty, Gerard (a family member of a friend in Ireland who tragically passed to spirit as a young boy), Anne, Steph, and Hazel (a long-time friend who had watched my children grow up until her sudden tragic passing in June 2007). All except for Jackie, Gerard, and Betty had met Mathew while they were on earth. Also present in spirit was Sarah, Rachel's grandmother, who had passed over the same year as Mum.

What a joy to have all of our loved ones present in spirit with us during this celebration!

Mum assured me that all the men in the family would be present on Saturday for the wedding.

Saturday came and it was a beautiful day. The sun was shining and a slight mist was in the background. The setting was fabulous and Rachel and Mathew had put such a lot of thought and attention into every detail of their wedding. They had even made the boutonnieres for the men from heather that they had collected en route to the Lake District and combined with gypsophilia and ribbon. It was decided that the women wouldn't wear corsages as they did not know the color of each of our outfits. On the top table there was even handpicked moss and heather, which symbolizes good luck, maternal love, and all wishes being granted.

There were more than forty guests in attendance at the service that was held in the banqueting hall at the Dale Lodge Hotel in Grasmere. As the service began I turned around to find that there were quite a few empty seats. Just as Rachel was being led by her father to the front to join Mathew, I again glanced at the seats and saw that they were occupied by our loved ones in spirit. There was Mum, Dad, Charlie and Anne, Johnnie, John Joe, Clifford and Betty (Mathew's great-granddad and great-grandma, and granddad Cyril from the Benson side of the family). Also present were Rachel's grandmother and granddad. Joining those gathered in spirit were Steph, Jackie, Hazel, and Gerard, all of whom represented loved ones from Ireland and England.

My tears started flowing and although I was so happy for Mathew and Rachel, I couldn't help but think if they only knew that our loved ones in spirit were also present to wish them well.

During the ceremony it was a great comfort to hear both Mathew and Rachel's dad mention these dear loved ones in spirit, thus honoring them and acknowledging their love even though they could not be physically present.

From beginning to end the day was filled with joy and laughter. Everyone played a part in the festivities. Marcus was best man and Elizabeth and Adam (Rachel's brother) signed the register. Then there were Rachel's three beautiful bridesmaids: Lisa, Vicky, and Claire, whom Rachel and Mathew had met while in university.

When the evening reception began, I took our grandsons, Lennon and Kenny, back to the cottage where they were staying so that it would give Elizabeth and Matt, her husband, some time together. When the children were settled and asleep, I started reminiscing about the day and said aloud, "I know that you all came today, but could I just have one sign that you are still here?"

No more than a half hour later, a white feather floated down from the ceiling to the floor and I picked it up. I didn't need any other words or signs of reassurance because I knew that my question had been answered.

CHAPTER 3
A Heavenly Home for Benson

Throughout my life pets have been a joy and a delight, as well as bringers of great sorrow when they became ill or injured and passed to spirit.

Now, just after Mum's passing, I was about to confront the loss of our very dearly loved dog, Benson, a black Labrador who had come into our family when he was just six weeks old.

It happened that one evening at around seven o'clock our grandson Lennon was with me in the living room watching television. There was nobody else in the house at the time. All of a sudden, Lennon touched his face and said, "What's this, Grandma?"

A white feather had drifted down and fallen onto his face. He picked it up and put it on the mantelpiece.

"It's only me," Mum said as she and Dad had a good chuckle.

Then Mum started to tell me about Lennon. She said that he was a gifted and talented child who would go far in life. She also told me that I should listen to my grandson as he always knew when she and Dad were around.

Meanwhile, Benson, who was with us in the room and who was very sensitive to the presence of spirits, started running around and looking up at the ceiling and this made me look up as well.

There in a corner of the living room I could clearly see that most of my family members who had passed on were seated around a long table. There were other people present in spirit as well that I did not recognize. Curious, I asked Mum who these people were. She explained that they were Dad's family who had lived in America and who had passed over. She said that she had just recently met them herself.

I had a full conversation out loud with Mum. Lennon kept looking at me in wonderment. Benson came and sat by my side to reassure me that no one was going to harm either of us. Benson laid his head on my lap and I stroked his fur. He gazed up at me almost as if to say that one day I would be looking up at the ceiling and seeing him there with the rest of my family.

The seasons turned over and we had a lovely spring and then summer was edging closer.

Marcus was awaiting the results of his A Levels, which would determine whether he was going to university or not.

Again, Mum came to reassure me that Marcus would do well in his exams.

When the results came, we were not disappointed. Marcus had gained a place at Manchester Metropolitan University to study Sports Science. Acceptance would, of course, mean that Marcus would be leaving home in September. Although I was very happy for him, I was also building myself up for when that time came because I knew how difficult it would be to let him go. I well remembered the time that our son Mathew left for university at the Glasgow School of Art and how long it took me to get used to him not being at home.

Daughter Elizabeth had only moved next door so she would always be around.

As the time drew closer for Marcus to leave, I noticed that Benson's health began to deteriorate. He was seen by the veterinarian, who diagnosed a brain tumor. It was very difficult to hear this as my brother Charlie had passed over with the same thing. The vet told me that Benson would probably get worse when Marcus left home as Benson had spent a lot of time with him.

My emotions were everywhere.

I now realized that things in my life happened in threes.

I explained Benson's condition to Marcus and he was very upset, as was the whole family. I reassured Marcus—who'd had Benson with him since he was four—that Benson would be taken great care of, but that the vet had the final decision. As a family we were all very much aware of how the possibility of Benson's passing was going to affect Marcus and so we tried not to mention the subject too often.

Benson had been given so much love during his time with our family, but saying now it was as if he knew that his time on earth was coming to an end and he seemed to accept this with peace and dignity.

$\sim$

Work, audiences, appointments, and church services kept me very busy and this was good because it kept my mind occupied.

Marcus now knew that he was moving into the Halls of Residence in Cheshire. The only drawback was that the halls were about two hours traveling distance from the university. However, Marcus had to take the offer as there was a shortage of rooms since so many students had qualified for the university.

We took Marcus to visit the halls and it seemed as if the place were in the middle of nowhere. We found out that the halls had actually been shut down but reopened to accommodate all the surplus students. I wasn't really worried about Marcus; it just seemed that he was so far away from home at this place.

Marcus moved out and into the Halls of Residence on Saturday, September 19, 2010. There were loads of tears as I realized that my baby had grown up. His bags and boxes were in the hallway waiting to be taken with him. There was so much stuff it took two vans to transport everything.

The house just felt so empty.

Benson was running around and I am sure that if dogs could speak he was saying "goodbye."

Marcus picked up a photograph of Benson to take with him and I remember him saying, "I'll see you next weekend, Benny."

We got Marcus settled in and Marcus's girlfriend, Nina, was very sad. She had been his girlfriend now for two years and, quite obviously, the distance apart was affecting both of them.

We got home and found Benson had become very distressed. He kept going up the stairs and sniffing in Marcus's room. He even climbed into Marcus's bed and laid his head on the pillow. I didn't have the heart to move him until later that night.

I also noticed that Benson hadn't eaten his dinner or drank any of his water. I was very worried. The vet was due to visit on Wednesday and, by this time, Benson had not eaten or drank his water since Sunday. I lay down with him and I talked to him. I knew that he understood. I said, "Benson, you are a dearly loved pet but I feel that the time has come to let you go." He just kept looking at me. I tried very hard to get him to eat or drink but he wasn't interested. I can't even remember him going to the toilet. He just kept pulling himself up the stairs and lying down outside Marcus's room. Marcus had been in touch but I just couldn't tell him what was happening even though he mentioned Benson a lot.

Wednesday came and the vet arrived. It was a different vet, not our usual one. Although she didn't know Benson very well, after her examination she thought that the best thing for Benson right now was for him to go to sleep.

The pain I felt within my heart was unbearable. I telephoned my daughter, Elizabeth, to see if she could come home from work just to be with me as Benson had been her dog originally. When she had left home he had come to stay with us. I suppose I was being selfish really, but I just didn't want to let go, especially with Mum's passing so recently in April, Marcus going to university, and now Benson.

Still, as I looked at Benson, I had the overwhelming feeling that he was happy to go.

$$\backsim$$

While I was waiting for Elizabeth to come home from work and the vet was gone to get all the supplies she needed from her surgery, as well as an extra nurse, I kept changing my mind. Part of my dilemma was that I would be leaving for

Ireland on Sunday and I couldn't bear the thought of not being with Benson when he passed.

Elizabeth arrived and we could have filled an ocean with our tears. We talked soothingly to Benson, telling him of the beautiful memories he had given our family and that we wanted him to know that he could never ever be replaced.

The vet and the nurse arrived. They had already telephoned the pet crematorium at Triangle, Sowerby Bridge and they were on their way to pick up Benson.

The vet was a young woman and she had already told me that she had a black Labrador of her own.

Elizabeth brought Benson in and the vet injected something into his leg to relax him. I knew there was no turning back then.

Benson just laid down and Elizabeth and I laid down with him. He just seemed so at peace. Then the vet gave him the final injection.

It was over in a matter of seconds. Everything was done with dignity as befitted a devoted and loving pet like Benson.

An hour later, Benson was taken from our home. I didn't know what type of vehicle had come for Benson, but when we went outside I saw that they had taken him in an animal hearse and I just thought how lovely that was.

There were some neighbors walking by at the time. They didn't say anything, just came over and held our hands and consoled us. They were also dog lovers and understood what we were going through.

Still raw with the grief of losing Benson, my thoughts turned to Marcus and I wondered how I was ever going to be able to tell him the sad news. I knew I would have to, of course, but I was trying to protect him from the loss of his faithful and loving pet.

I didn't call Marcus but he phoned us on Wednesday evening to check on Benson. I paused and Kenn persuaded me to tell him so that he would be aware of what he was coming home to. After I told Marcus there was a great silence and then I could hear his heartbreaking sobs. I felt so badly that I wasn't there to comfort him. We talked for a while and Marcus said that deep down he had known when he left that he would never see Benson alive again and that was why, in his quieter moments, he had taken time to say goodbye to his devoted companion.

Benson's ashes were returned to us and the lady from the crematorium asked me if I would like an inscription on his casket and these were the words that came to me:

"Benson, you are now in heaven, where you can freely roam, but you will be so dearly missed by all of us back home."

Benson's ashes now sit on the mantelpiece in the dining room with his photograph on top.

After I posted the news of Benson's death on my website, so many people had memories of him to share. There were stories about how he used to lick them to death and also how he would run around the house and let us know when people were coming to visit. He was always able to see the spirit people that visitors brought with them and acknowledged their presence as well. I also had my own sweet remembrances—like the time one of our children gave him a red neckerchief, or how he greeted the postman each day. When he was younger and Elizabeth was still living at home, he used to know what bus she was coming home on. He would run around and wait at the door for her to open it and then he would be all over her.

It was a great comfort to me to have these memories as well as the ones shared with me by guests, friends, and people on the website. I was very grateful that Benson had shared thirteen years of his life with us. Thankfully, we had captured much of Benson's life in photos and on film

Dear Benson had seen all three of our children leave home and had been there when Lennon had come into our family. He had even shared Mum's last Christmas with us. I smiled at one of the memories of that Christmas day: I remember how well I thought she was eating her Christmas dinner until I found out that she had been feeding Benson who was underneath the table!

I knew Mum would be glad to see him again.

Kenn and I went to pick up Marcus on Thursday and bring him home. I could see how sad he looked and he just hugged me. He was crying so much and wondering if Benson died because he had left home. I told him the truth— that yes, Benson did seem to be looking for him all the time. I also reminded him that the vet had said that when he left home for university we would notice a change in Benson. I just never realized that it would be so quick.

Marcus talked about how he felt about his grandma's passing, moving out of home, and now Benson. Even Kenn was very emotional and he is not one to easily show his feelings.

I knew with great certainty that Benson would be back in spirit and I didn't have long to wait.

That night, sure enough, we could all hear those big paws pounding down the staircase.

None of us were scared as we knew exactly who it was.

⁓

There had been pets before Benson—seven cats over the years.

One of the last two cats, a tabby named Madeline, was a beautiful, sensitive cat that only went out to use the toilet. She was very much an at-home cat and used to sleep a lot on my side of the bed—much to the disapproval of Kenn. She followed me everywhere and always made such a fuss when I had to be away from home. She seemed more like a small child that needed constant reassurance from her mother.

I will never forget the morning that Kenn, Marcus, and I went on holiday to Cyprus at the end of July 2006. My mother-in-law came to stay at the house and look after the cats while we were away. This was mainly because I never wanted to put them in either a cattery or a kennel.

On the evening of our first day on holiday, I thought it strange that while we were in the restaurant a tabby cat came to our table. The cat just seemed to come out of nowhere. My first thought was wondering if Madeline and the rest of the pets were okay. Later I asked the restaurant owner if the tabby cat belonged to him. He replied that he had never seen a cat in the restaurant.

My thoughts and concerns got the better of me and I just couldn't shake the feeling that something was wrong with Madeline. I sent a text to Mathew via Kenn's mobile phone, only to receive a text back the next day saying Madeline had been missing for nearly two days. She hadn't come back in since Nana had let her out to go to the toilet on the day we left for our holiday.

Instinctively I knew there was going to be bad news.

A few nights later we went to a different restaurant which was down a lane and, as we were walking, a tabby cat came up to meet us and brushed beside my leg. I thought it strange as there were other people walking down the lane to the same restaurant and the cat never went near any of them. I realized that it was Madeline coming back to me in spirit to let me know that she had passed.

Although I enjoyed the holiday with my family, my mind cast back to the morning we left home. Madeline was in the corridor and she ran and jumped up on my shoulder. She was really purring and rubbing her head up against my face. I wondered if this had somehow been her way of telling me that she wouldn't be there when we returned home.

After two weeks we got back home. The first thing I did was put down my suitcase and go to search for Madeline. I went to ask the neighbors if anyone had seen her. I was told by one neighbor that he had seen a lady come into the yard and pick up a tabby cat but as he wasn't sure the cat was Madeline, he didn't say anything to her. The lady lived on the street above mine and I found out that she had stolen Madeline. Another neighbor told me that a tabby cat was killed outside a shop—on what would turn out to be Madeline's thirteenth birthday.

I was devastated.

I put a notice in all the local papers and three weeks later, while I was out shopping, a friend and colleague of mine, from when I was a nurse, told me that she had seen the letter in the paper and didn't have the heart to ring me to tell me that it was her son who had knocked Madeline down and killed her. Madeline was apparently attempting to make her way back home and away from the lady who had taken her. As Madeline was not used to the main road, she jumped in front of the car. There was no chance of Madeline being saved. The young man did take Madeline away and buried her where he had laid his own cats to rest. Madeline was buried close to the Moorcock Inn at Norland. It was a beautiful spot where people go to picnic and to walk. I felt that at last I could let go of Madeline as I knew she had a lovely final resting place.

We also had Holly, a black cat who had been a stray. Holly used to just turn up at the door, meowing all the time. She looked unkempt and I eventually persuaded her to come into our home. Three weeks later she gave birth to three kittens on Elizabeth's bed. The kittens were absolutely beautiful—gray with speckled spots. They looked like baby leopards! Kenn was not amused as the house was being taken over by animals. I said to him, "Cats choose their home and, obviously, ours is the one where Holly has chosen to have her babies."

We found homes for the kittens so we were just left with Holly and made sure that she didn't have any more babies.

We had Holly for twelve years but found that, after Madeline had gone, she seemed to deteriorate. One day as I came into the dining room, she was obviously distraught and in pain and she kept falling over. I got her to the vet who told me that Holly had had a stroke. I was given some medication for the cat. Two days later Holly was again suffering from the same ailment. There was no alternative but to have her go to sleep. It was a very hard and heart-wrenching decision. I had grown to dearly love Holly. There were no further animals until Benson.

We all decided, as a family, that after all the pain and emotion we had felt at the passing of Benson there would never be another pet in our house. It was a very tough decision to make, but not one of us thought we could ever again endure the heartache that comes with the loss of a beloved pet. We do not have any more pets as I cannot bear the pain of loving and then losing them. Now we have a bird table and enjoy watching the birds eat and wash and flutter about outdoors—for me this is very therapeutic.

I love all birds but when the robin comes I feel that is spirit's way of saying "thank you" for looking after the birds.

~⁄∘

We had a lovely weekend with Marcus and he delighted in telling us all about the Halls of Residence and what was expected of him at university. He would be returning back on Sunday—the same day that I was flying to Ireland.

I wondered how Kenn would feel being alone in an empty house.

Monday morning, just before I was about to start my appointments in Ireland, I had a phone call from Kenn. He told me that he had heard and seen Benson coming down the stairs just before he set off for work. He thought it was best that he didn't shut the doors so Benson's spirit could still find his way around the home. It was unusual for Kenn to tell me this, as—although he believes fully in my work and supports me—he never speaks a great deal about hearing or seeing anything from the spirit world. However, as he related seeing Benson's spirit I could hear the emotion in his voice. I reassured him that old faithful Benson was still doing his job of protecting and guarding the home.

Throughout the two weeks that I was away, Kenn told me in conversations that Benson visited every single night. I felt happy with that, but at the same time I thought that he should rest.

I was kept busy with appointments but, somehow, the appointments this time were presenting with lots of tragedies of different kinds: suicide, tragic accidents, disease—and I realized anew how many people were reaching out for comfort and reassurance that the spirit world did exist. I found myself delving much deeper into my work to try to help people make contact with their departed loved ones. Many people were questioning why such awful things happened and, if there was a God, surely he would try and prevent these things from happening. I had to think carefully as to how to answer these questions. I sent my thoughts out to spirit and what came back to me was: "How is it that everyone blames God when things go wrong? Believe in him and accept that life challenges all of us at some time. Even if we feel that he has deserted us when we need him the most, that is often when he is there for us more than ever." Spirit also told me that we should all take personal responsibility for our actions.

Before I left for England I felt that it was really necessary to visit Mum's only surviving relative, John Knight. Although John seemed okay, he did ask me when I was returning to Ireland again. I told him that it would be late November. He said, "That will be too late. I will have gone." I hugged him and I didn't say anything, but for the first time ever I felt that what he had said was going to come true.

John passed to spirit on November 2—another prediction that came to pass.

Kenn and I would return to Ireland for John's funeral and I have to say he looked absolutely beautiful. Mary, his daughter, had him dressed in a new suit, laid out on his bed, and I couldn't help thinking how much he looked like Mum—and so young, even though he was eighty-nine. I asked him to take a message to Mum and felt at ease that all the ones from that generation were now reunited. I felt as if a great deal of my time was being spent on and off airplanes through both work and bereavement, but that was how my life was obviously meant to be.

The days passed quickly and I couldn't believe that we were coming to the end of another year. Now all my thoughts had turned to the preparation of the Christmas holidays with the realization that this year there would be no Mum and no Benson there to celebrate with us.

Christmas morning came and with a heavy heart I was setting the table for dinner and waiting for Billy to arrive. Everyone was doing their own thing. We had been around to Elizabeth's house to see Lennon open his presents. He was so happy as he was just about the age to understand about Santa and also about what Christmas meant.

The Christmas music was playing in the background as Kenn was preparing dinner. The dining room looked lovely.

I sent out a message to Mum and Dad and my family in spirit asking them to give me the strength to get through the day when suddenly I looked at the dining room table and there Mum was! She said, "Don't be sad, Bridget. You know where I am. I can show you where we all are and who is with us."

"Okay, Mum," I said. "Do that."

What I saw I will never forget.

All of my family known to me were seated in a garden surrounded with trees containing fruits and flowers. In the distance I could see a clear blue sky and also the sea. Right at the side of Mum was our beloved Benson and Mum was feeding him. His bowl was full and his food looked yummy and he certainly was enjoying it.

Mum said, "Look, that's the Benson you know."

He looked absolutely beautiful and healthy. For a few moments I just stepped outside of myself and joined them. I wondered how I could ever wish them back on earth.

From then on the dark cloud that had seemed to hover over me lifted and we went on to have a wonderful Christmas Day with family and friends who came over in the evening.

Billy didn't mention Mum throughout the day but I talked to him about her.

He just said, "As long as I know that she is okay, I can deal with that."

∽◯

There have been several occasions when the enduring spirit of an animal has proven to me and to others that a beloved pet does not simply cease to be, but, just like their human counterparts, passes on to heaven.

One of these remarkable incidents involved my friend, Dawn.

Dawn had a beautiful cocker spaniel named Jack. Benson and Jack were the best of friends and Dawn and I often went walking with the dogs at least twice a week in the park and along the canal. The dogs loved to play and cavort with one another and it was a delight to watch them together.

One day we noticed that Jack didn't seem to be his usual cheerful self when he came to visit us—and Benson seemed to notice this as well. Even though the two dogs greeted one another, they weren't as playful as before. Dawn took Jack to the vet to be examined and the diagnosis came back that he had a brain tumor.

Jack went to his eternal sleep on New Year's Eve, 2008.

Dawn and her family were devastated. They had lost not only a family pet but also a best friend.

When Dawn came to see me again, Benson seemed to know that it was her car that had pulled up outside and he began running up and down the corridor expecting Jack to be with her.

As soon as Dawn got to the door, both Benson and I could plainly see that Jack was with her—but from spirit. He came in with her and after Benson had a cuddle with

Dawn he came to lay down at my feet. He looked up at me as if to say, "I have lost my best friend."

Dawn and I hugged one another and both of us burst into tears. We had memories of Jack to share through photographs but I had to pause and consider not only how sad it was for Dawn, but also how I would feel when that day came for Benson.

A year passed and Dawn's son, Richard, bought her another cocker spaniel who was named Oscar. He is an absolutely beautiful dog and she loves him but, as she says, he will never replace Jack.

❦

At one time I looked after an older lady named Irene. Irene was a real lady who had wined and dined with royalty. She told me that one of her best friends had been Winston Churchill, and she had photographs on her wall of the two of them together.

Irene was somewhat of a recluse at the time I was caring for her but she had company in the form of a Yorkshire terrier named George, who was her dearest friend.

I used to take dinner to Irene every day and we would sit and visit about times gone by. She had had many businesses throughout her life and always had kept dogs, mainly Alsatians, but it was easier for her at that point in her life to care for a small dog like George.

George was very protective and caring of Irene, as I observed on a few occasions.

Irene liked to have a good tipple of red wine now and again and there were times when I arrived at her home to find that she had fallen or collapsed. George was there beside her, whining as if he was trying to alert someone of Irene's plight.

One morning Irene let George out onto the grass near her home, but sadly he somehow wandered onto the busy main road and was knocked down by a car. The car did not stop but George made his way back home. He had dragged himself by his two front paws. Irene rang the vet as she did not want to disturb me and the vet came out. Little George passed away in Irene's arms.

After George's passing Irene became a total recluse, but she did tell me that George visited her in spirit—often lying on her bed every night.

Irene made the decision that many pet owners do when a dearly loved animal companion passes into spirit—she decided that she would not have another dog. She did, however, get a black male cat that had only three legs. She named him Manx. Manx was just as good a protector and caretaker of Irene as George had been and, until he got to know me, was somewhat challenging to get past when I brought her meals across.

Irene had Manx with her until her passing in January 2007. Her nephew then took Manx and although I do not know for sure, I feel that Manx passed into spirit soon after Irene.

⟋⟍

A great many of the clients who come to see me have lost dear animal companions and these pets are not limited to cats and dogs—there are also those who have lost horses, birds, and all types of creatures that are precious to them. They seek reassurance that somehow these pets have survived physical death and are now in a place of light, health, and happiness.

I very much love to see the look on a client's face when a departed pet comes through, giving comfort and proof that their sweet souls also survive and reside in heaven.

CHAPTER 4

Some Special Sessions

Every one of my sessions is very special and I feel so blessed to be able to share my gift with those who come to me seeking comfort and hope. To be able to help the people who come through my door find healing and peace after the passing to spirit of a loved one or a pet makes me so grateful. As a channel between the two worlds, I feel it is a privilege to be able to give both evidence and comfort to people who are grieving, or who may be facing their own mortality.

I also strongly believe that we are all able to communicate with departed loved ones via our thoughts and, if we are patient, those who have passed over will answer our questions and concerns. However, in order for this communication to take place with the spirit world, we have to have an open mind and a heart that does not judge and is accepting. We must *believe*, and if we do, then the answers will come.

In the past when I had sessions with my clients I always found that no two days were the same. However, more recently, I have found that I am dealing with some terrible tragedies and passings. When a client sits in front of me I never know until I start the reading how it is going to go, but again, through all of 2011 and so far into 2012 I have noted that many of those passing to spirit are young.

Nicola

One of these very special people was a young girl named Nicola whose mum came to me for a reading.

Nicola would come to be known around the world because of the courage she displayed after being diagnosed with an inherited condition known as giant axonal neuropathy. This condition involves the dysfunction of a specific type of protein in nerve cells (neurons). These proteins are essential for normal nerve function. Nicola would not be properly diagnosed until she was seven years of age.

I had known Nicola since she was about four years of age. At the time when her mum, Breege, came for a reading with Nicola in January of 1990, Nicola was approaching her fourth birthday in July. I remember saying to Breege that "I only wish I could grant miracles" as I could see from the reading that Nicola wouldn't have a long life. Breege had carried Nicola in her arms to my home and a friend took care of Nicola while Breege was having the reading. I knew that because of her condition Nicola could hardly walk.

Being a mother myself, I found this reading very difficult as I had to explain to Nicola's mum that there was never going to be a cure, but I would give Nicola some healing that day and continue to send healing out to her.

I had an extremely emotional time of it when I held Nicola on my knee and talked to her while I was giving her the healing. Even though she was only four years old, she seemed to have total comprehension of what I was saying.

I also gave Nicola a very special aquamarine crystal to keep to aid her in her healing. The crystal, known for its ability to impart courage and Calm, is one that I had, for some reason, recently purchased for myself—something I had never done before. While I was with Nicola I realized that the real reason I had purchased the crystal was so that I could give it to her.

Nicola came into my home being carried, and walked out on her own.

My own daughter, Elizabeth, was just nine at the time of Nicola's visit. In gratefulness I hugged her tightly with tears streaming down my face. She asked me what was wrong and I remember saying that if I could have one wish it was that Nicola would be able to grow up and be a mum one day. But I knew that was not to be.

As I was trying to explain everything to Elizabeth there was a knock on the door. Nicola had returned and she stood there holding her mum's hand. She could see that I had been crying and she asked me why. I tried to make an excuse but somehow the words wouldn't come. She took hold of my hand and said, "I will treasure this crystal that you have given me. Don't be sad as the angels are not coming for me yet."

After Nicola and her mum had left for the second time and even though I felt a great connection to the child, I promised myself that I wouldn't keep in touch because if I felt so much pain now, what would I feel when her time came?

How very wrong could I be?

In July of that year I attended the Irish Festival at The Piece Hall in Halifax. The Piece Hall is a historic building with open-air fetes and markets. About four thousand people were in attendance on that lovely day. Suddenly I heard a voice calling my name and when I turned around I saw Nicola in a wheelchair and her mum was with her. I thought, "Oh my God, what am I going to do?" Then I heard my father's voice saying, "This is meant to be, Bridget. She is a beautiful child and if you can help her or her parents in any way that is what I want you to do." I said, "Okay," and went to give Nicola a really big hug. Then I asked her how she had managed to find me in such a big crowd and she said, "I just did." That was enough for me to know that we could never, ever lose contact.

I continued to see Nicola and her parents, Breege and David. They both came from Irish backgrounds so we would always meet at various functions.

Nicola's life was full of love and happiness and she was brought up in a calm environment. She had one brother, Gary, who was older than her. I often wondered about him and how he was coping in the midst of everything that was happening to his sister.

Toward the last three months of Nicola's life, just a few months from her twenty-fourth birthday, Nicola was in the hospital.

Kenn and I went to see her one week before she passed. Although we had visited her many times before that, the last week I knew would be my final visit. She was so painfully thin but she put her arms around me as best as she could. She said, "I am glad you have come, Bridget and Kenn. Next week I am going home." I knew what she meant but didn't want to say too much at that time. There was another gentleman visiting her as well that day and I just looked up at him and both his eyes and Kenn's welled up with tears.

Nicola caught a glimpse and she asked them both why they were upset. Neither one could answer her. She said, "Don't be sad, be happy. I've had a great life and I am going home."

Nicola turned to me and said, "I have seen where I am going, Bridget. It's absolutely beautiful."

She asked me if there was anyone with her from spirit and I said, "Yes." There were two animals with her: a cat that she had lost and her friend Avril's goat that had gone to spirit. I had given the goat healing but sadly the animal had been put to sleep as there had been no cure for its illness.

Nicola smiled at me so brightly when she heard this news. Then she asked, "Is there anyone else?"

I said, "Yes."

I described the spirit of a young man in his forties who was by her side, and I knew he was the one who would look after her and take her home.

Nicola was very happy to hear this. "That's my uncle, John Joe!"

John Joe had passed to spirit recently and Nicola's ashes would be taken home to Ireland to be buried in the same grave as John Joe.

Nicola had already chosen the song she wanted played at her funeral—"You're My Best Friend"—a song that had been recorded onto a CD and sung by her uncles.

She also asked me if I knew what outfit she would be wearing for her funeral and I said, "It will be pink."

I could see that she was getting tired and by this time the emotional pain was starting to pull at my heart and all I could pray was that God would give Breege, David, and Gary strength when the time came.

I told Nicola that we were leaving. She asked where her mum was and I told her that she was outside speaking with a nurse. She asked if I could have her mum come in to be with her and when Breege came into the room Nicola, with a faint breath, asked her mum to give both Kenn and me a hug to say thank you for all the years I had been there for her. She told her mum what she had told me.

After Breege had given Kenn and me final hugs, we went outside and Breege joined us. She said, "I know it's very near, Bridget. Will she be okay?" I said, "Yes. She will. We have to let her go. She knows where she is going and she is not sad."

Breege then asked me if I thought that Nicola might be able to make it home to Huddersfield. I paused and then carefully said, "I am sorry but that wish can't be granted."

Nicola passed away the following Tuesday, April 19, 2011 in the arms of her parents and brother.

Nicola's funeral would not be held until May 3 due to the Easter holidays. Kenn and I attended the service. Breege told us that it was Nicola's wish that everyone attending the funeral wear something pink, as that was her favorite color.

Because we were very nearly like family, Kenn and I were invited to Huddersfield to wait for Nicola to return home one final time. We all stood outside and soon, around the corner came two shire horses, pulling what looked like a Cinderella carriage. Inside the carriage was Nicola's pink coffin. The horses had pink plumes and everything was pink, even the butterflies on the coffin.

There was near silence and all we could hear was the steady "clip, clop" of the horses' hooves.

Suddenly Breege let out a wail. We could all hear her say, "Oh, my baby, my baby!"

Gary and David went forward to console her, even though they were crying themselves.

I took hold of Breege's hand and said, "Remember, Breege, what Nicola told us—that she was not sad. She was very happy to be going to her new home."

I truly didn't know what else to say at that moment as my own heart was breaking too. During her short time on earth Nicola had been given so much love and care by her family and friends and now each one of us had to accept and let her go. And even though I knew exactly where Nicola was going, I had to pause and consider how her family was feeling.

Everyone gathered together and we all walked slowly behind the coffin until we got to the end of her street. Neighbors stood on doorsteps saluting her as this is an Irish tradition.

Another old Irish tradition is that all the curtains in a home are closed as a mark of respect to the departed, and I noticed that this had been done in all the houses along the street.

We returned to our car and followed the cortege. Many of the local people continued to walk, forming a procession to the church. I thought how lovely it was that no other cars overtook us.

When we arrived at the church it was absolutely heaving with people and by the time we got inside there were no seats left. Glancing around, I noted that everyone was wearing something pink in honor of Nicola. Many of us were standing. One thing I noticed was that a beautiful butterfly flew in the door, circled around Nicola's coffin, and then flew back out again.

Nicola had gained worldwide fame, not only because of her illness, but also for her courage. Everyone she met fell in love with her. She never complained or asked why she was stricken with this rare disease, but accepted and shone a light for many who were struggling with their own health issues.

After Nicola's body was handed over for cremation, her family released pink balloons into the sky and then everyone joined together at the Irish Club in Huddersfield for a celebration of Nicola's life. There was food, alcohol, and even a band. That was what Nicola had wanted and she certainly got her wish. It was both difficult and heartening to see Nicola's family and so many young people of Nicola's age present and coming to terms with the loss of such a beautiful person.

Kenn and I will never forget Nicola or her family. Often I wonder if I would have ever crossed paths with Nicola had I not been given the gift bestowed on me when I was three years of age—ironically the same age as Nicola when she and her mum came to see me for the first time.

Just after Nicola's funeral—about a week later—Nicola came through to me and these are the words she gave me to put into a poem:

Two angels came to the side of my bed
You look tired, both of them said
We have come to take you home,
Making sure you're not alone.
I have a mum and dad and a brother too
I wonder what they are going to do
They want me to stay on earth
They have loved me dearly
Since my birth.
I know my time on earth is done
And that's the reason you've both come
Please give me strength to help me through
In all the things I have to do.
To Mum and Dad I want to say
I love you both more each day
And to my brother, my number one
Thanks for your love and all you've done.
To all I am going to leave behind
You're never going to be far from my mind
I'm not scared, so please don't cry
I know that this is not goodbye.
My life on earth was never sad
So fulfilled with all I had
My family always by my side
And friends I made from far and wide.
All these memories I will treasure
In my eternal home forever
Keep wearing pink and you will see
You're never far away from me.

After this Nicola also made her presence known to family members. Breege told me that as she left the funeral home just prior to the funeral service she had experienced a very strong smell of Nicola's perfume all around her. She felt very reassured that Nicola was letting her know that she was okay.

Nicola, like many spirits who pass, was also able to let her family know she was present by dimming or turning lights off and on. This is a very well-documented way those in spirit use to communicate. One of the first of these instances occurred when the family had been specifically speaking about Nicola's burial and funeral in Ireland (on July 20). During that conversation the lights dimmed or blew out.

Nicola's father, Dave, and Breege's brother, Frank, also had experiences that to them proved the presence of Nicola. One beautiful morning after Nicola's passing, the family decided to have breakfast outside. Breege brought out the teapot, cups, and cutlery as well as a bottle of brown sauce on the tray that Nicola had always used for her meals. Frank and Dave were talking about Nicola when suddenly the bottle of brown sauce moved from one end of the tray to the other all by itself! Dave was certain that it was Nicola letting them know she could hear them.

Another instance occurred one day when Dave was at his sister Sandra's home. Dave's good friend, Anne, was also there. Everyone was seated around the breakfast bar and Anne asked how the family was coping after Nicola's death. Suddenly one of the lights above the breakfast bar went out. Dave said that it was Nicola again, letting them all know that she was around. Anne commented that it could have been anything that caused the light to go out, but wouldn't it be good if the light turned itself back on again—and yes, lo and behold, it did!

My own experiences with Nicola after she passed came in the form of messages. The main theme of these messages has been her hope that I will look after her Mum, Dad, and brother. She seems delighted that she no longer needs to use a wheelchair to get around and she has no difficulty speaking or communicating as she did when she was alive. When she was on earth she had a very difficult time getting her words out and I felt that sometimes people who did not really know her dismissed her and did not take the time to understand what she was trying to say. All of her friends were wonderful through the years and they stood by her. Nicola once told me, "People look through me as if I am not there. I am just the same as they are. It's just that I need a wheelchair to get around. My mind is sound and first impressions are lasting impressions."

Another indication to me was that after Nicola's passing I found that more and more someone would walk through the door wearing pink. As that was Nicola's favorite color I knew that whenever I saw the color pink that was Nicola being by my side.

I couldn't have loved Nicola more if she were my own daughter.

Nicola remains in close contact with me from spirit to this day.

My Sister-in-Law, Steph

My sister-in-law, Steph, had been a bridesmaid at my wedding and was also a great friend of mine.

She was married to Kenn's brother, David, in October 1982, and the couple settled in Illingworth, Halifax. Steph was very spiritual and always told me about the presence of spirits in their home in Illingworth. I recall one day that I visited her for lunch. I had to use the bathroom, which was located in the upstairs of the house. On my way up the stairs I was met by a spirit man. He was dressed in a Quaker's outfit and I tried to pass him by, but there was no way that he was going to let me do so. He made me go back downstairs and he also came down with me. I asked him his name and he declined to give it to me, but he did say that he had lived in the house previously and that he wasn't happy that so much work had been done on the home. (David had knocked down several walls, which had changed the whole appearance of the home.) The spirit said that he preferred that the place remain as it had been in the past.

Back downstairs I mentioned the spirit to Steph and she told me that she had seen him on several occasions and that she felt protected by him, but I did not share that same feeling.

I went back upstairs to the bathroom before I left and here was the spirit man once again. I felt very intimidated by his presence. He spoke and told me that his name was Thomas Samuel (he did not give me his surname) and I now felt a little less afraid of him. I asked him what was the purpose of him being in the home and he told me that it was to protect Steph, both in and out of the house. This protectiveness seemed to be because he knew she was a nurse and that it was a concern to him that she looked after ill people. He also told me that Steph's husband David created a bad energy within the house as he was drinking heavily and that this would have an immensely negative effect on their marriage.

When I told Steph about this conversation, she did open up and say that she felt that David had a problem with drinking but he wouldn't admit to it.

There was also a spirit lady who made several appearances throughout the day. She was dressed in clothing of the Victorian era and she always seemed to be baking. She told me her name was Anastasia. A spirit who spent time baking fit in quite well with Steph as she also enjoyed baking. That very day of my visit Steph had made Hungarian goulash for lunch and it was very tasty.

I asked Steph what she thought about having so many spirits visiting the home. She said that she was quite happy to have them around, but she wanted me to explain to them that she worked nights and that she didn't want to be disturbed by them during the day when she was resting from a twelve-hour night shift. She also said that Thomas Samuel smoked cigars and that she didn't like the smell in the house. I passed her messages on to Anastasia and Thomas Samuel and from that day onward they only came to visit her on her return from work. The spirits respected Steph and her schedule and left her to her rest. Thomas Samuel also stopped smoking cigars in Steph's home.

I think that Steph was very pleased when I told her that the spirits were not there to harm her, but rather were there to protect her.

Steph and David moved from the house at Illingworth, Halifax two years later to a house in Boothtown, still in the Halifax area. David once again completely renovated this new home. This brought many spirits to visit, especially spirit children. There were at least four of them, two boys and two girls, and they told me that they had been born in the house over a hundred years earlier. The boys were dressed in long shorts with braces and gingham checked shirts. They also wore clogs on their feet and peaked caps. The girls were dressed in beautiful dresses, which had bibs attached to them. They wore ankle socks and they had shiny patent leather shoes on their feet. They also showed me that they would wear hats that matched their dresses whenever they went out to church or any special occasion. I sensed they were a strongly religious family, although I never saw the parents. The boys were called Harry and Clement and the girls' names were Beatrice and Harriet. They all seemed to suit their names very well.

The children were regular visitors to Steph's home and it was in that house that she conceived her only child, Daniel, who is now twenty-six years of age. Even he, as a child, commented that he had some imaginary friends who visited and he didn't seem at all disturbed by this.

Steph and David stayed in the house at Boothtown for about four years, and then moved to their third and final house as a married couple. They would divorce soon after due to irreconcilable differences. I remember my visits to Steph afterward and always found the house to be totally peaceful with beautiful energy surrounding it.

Steph lived in the marital home until she met and married her second husband, Martin, and they moved to another house, where she lived until she passed to spirit after a long battle with cancer.

Daniel still lives in that house today as Steph willed it to him after her death. I am sure he still very much senses her presence as he recalls the many wonderful memories of their time shared together. I must remark that Steph had been for many readings with other people who always saw a different life for her from the one I had seen. And, it should also be noted that Steph shied away from the truth about her condition and refused to accept the reality of it. Prior to her passing we talked a great deal about her impending death and she told me, "I'm not really sure if the spirit world does exist as I am having to leave behind my family and my only child." I told her that I totally accepted what she was saying but that I also wanted to make a pact with her. I suggested that after she passed and when she was ready that perhaps she could come through another medium and communicate with me.

Time went by and then three years after Steph had passed to spirit I was at my local Spiritualist church. There was a male medium there that day—someone I had never seen before. At the end of the service he said, "I need to come to the lady at the back of the church, dressed in a blue jacket." This was me and I responded that it was fine.

The medium told me that he had a young lady with him with icy blue eyes and a lovely smile. He said that she had told him that she had passed over with cancer and the only word she gave him was "Popeye." I couldn't speak as I knew that Steph had had a parrot named Popeye. No one else would have ever known that and although it was just one word, it reassured me that she had communicated.

I still feel Steph's presence around me and I always include her in any celebrations that we may have as a family.

Ironically, my daughter Elizabeth's baby was due on Steph's birthday, June 25, 2012. And although the new baby could never replace Steph, I know it brings comfort and joy to both families that the baby and Steph, who was Elizabeth's godmother, will share their birthdays.

Sam

Another experience was when I received a telephone call from a young woman named Sam. Sam shared a house with three other girls and she said that there was the spiritual presence of a lady and also a man at the house and that she felt they were somehow linked to one another.

Sam was very interested in the spirit world and she wanted me to find out who these spirits were. I went to visit the home one Sunday morning as this was the only time that I had free. I took with me a member of my local Spiritualist church, Ron Paul, as I wasn't sure what kind of spirit I would be dealing with. I felt it was better that I would have the energy of another person who knew how to protect themselves and the home.

Three of the girls who lived at the home were there when we arrived. Two of them seemed very worried. I went around all the rooms and the spirit lady I found to be present was Sam's late mother, who had only recently passed over. I connected with her and she told me to make Sam aware that it was just her and that there was no need for her to worry. She also said that it was her wish to be able to visit Sam on a regular basis. When told this, Sam became very emotional and was elated that her mum had found her way back to the house. Sam was also very agreeable to her mum visiting more often.

What came next took me by surprise as I found that one of the girls I had tuned into, Angela, used the Ouija board in her bedroom to contact a male friend of hers, Andrew, who had committed suicide by jumping in front of a train. Angela had a photograph of Andrew taken of him in his coffin and when she had contacted Andrew she had placed this in the center of the Ouija board.

I made contact with Andrew and he told me that he was earthbound, which means that he couldn't move to the light that would enable him to pass to spirit. He was bound to the earth and unable to move forward because Angela could not let go of him. She had not realized that by using the Ouija board so soon after his passing that, unfortunately, she was keeping him from making his transition. It was Andrew's wish that he be set free so that he could move on to his eternal life as he had been and was unhappy on earth and his unhappiness was what had caused him to take his own life.

I had to explain all of this to Angela as well as the others who were present. At first Angela denied that she had used the Ouija board, but eventually she admitted that this was the case. That was when she showed us the photograph of Andrew in his coffin. I asked for her permission to send Andrew into the light and on to spirit and she agreed. I explained what was going to happen. After this we all sat and prayed as we would have done at a funeral. We had left both the front and the back doors open wide for Andrew's spirit to be able to leave the house. I told the girls that Andrew could walk out of either door or there was the possibility that another spirit would come to help him in his transition. This is the way I had been taught to release earthbound spirits.

After about ten minutes of prayer Andrew was ready to leave.

The only way I can describe what happened next is that it was as if a tornado of light took place. Andrew was in the middle of the light and I could see his red hair and blue eyes. He was wearing jeans and a beige sweater with a white shirt underneath it. I could see nothing on his feet.

The tornado of light filled the entire area from Angela's bedroom and on down the stairs. It went on through the lounge and then out of the front door. We could all see and feel the presence of Andrew leaving the home and although it was very emotional for Angela as she was the only one of us who had actually known Andrew, it was a relief for the rest of the girls who lived there.

The force of that tornado of light was very powerful and I felt that, when it was over, Andrew was at peace and very happy that his transition had finally taken place.

When everything was calm again, I spoke to the girls and explained the danger of using the Ouija board without the experience, protection, and knowledge of what it entails. During this time I got the distinct feeling that the energy from Angela was not a positive one and that she enjoyed contacting spirits of any kind, good or bad. I also told Angela that Andrew would not be coming back through use of the Ouija board again and that if she wanted to contact him, I would be quite happy to help her make that connection.

I never heard from Angela again but I heard from the other girls that she had moved out of the house soon after Andrew's transition.

The other girls are now settled with their partners in different homes.

Lisa and Penny

Often, with this gift, I never know what someone's fate will be. This happened to our family on November 25, 2011 with the untimely passing of my sister-in-law, Lisa. Lisa lived with her family in Grimsby, East Yorkshire. Her mum, Penny, had moved to Cleethorpes some years after the passing of Lisa's dad, Cyril. Although they were very close and best friends, after Lisa had her first heart attack on May 19, 2011, everything changed. Lisa became withdrawn and I suppose she felt that her life was never the same after that. Her mum was always a strong person and seemed to push her own thoughts onto Lisa, telling her that she should just get on with her life. Lisa and Penny had a fallout, which sadly was never resolved. At the beginning of November, I had a message from my late father-in-law that there was an impending passing and that it would be Lisa. He wanted me to try and help Penny and Lisa resolve their differences as it would be too late once Lisa passed. I had to pass the message from his father on to my husband, Kenn. We then both tried to help Penny and Lisa resolve things, but neither one made any attempt to settle the issues between them. So, sadly, Lisa passed with no reconciliation. I can't begin to express the pain I felt when this happened as I knew that spirit had not been listened to and now it was too late. This incident with Lisa and Penny has made me realize more than ever that no matter how bad an argument or misunderstanding is, it is always best to try and make up. I am sure that Lisa has now put the past behind her. Her mum's heart is still broken in two and, although she has not said it yet, I know that Lisa has been back to her as she has visited me several times. The only thing Lisa has ever said to me is: "Please look after my children and thank you for always mentioning my name. I am with Dad and I will remain here until we are all reunited one day."

Shirley

Shirley, one of my regular clients and a very spiritual lady, has always been at hand to help everyone else.

Shirley did not have a loving relationship with her parents, who had both passed to spirit. When she came for a reading with me she was quite shocked that her parents came through to ask her for forgiveness.

Shirley refused to accept their presence, much less their request for forgiveness. I had to admit that I was taken aback as I was trying to listen to everything her parents were saying, and yet, at the same time, I had to accept that Shirley had the right to refuse their request. I found myself in the dilemma of telling the parents that Shirley did not want to continue with the reading if they were going to stay.

I took the step of asking Shirley why she did not want her parents present throughout the reading and her words to me were, "I don't even want to remember them in any way, shape, or form." She told me that she would appreciate it if I would not approach the subject again.

This is one example of a client not accepting that even though family members can sometimes be cruel while here on earth, they do see things differently when they pass over to spirit. To them forgiveness is very important so that they can move on in their eternal life.

As for Shirley's parents, I can only hope that they are happy where they are, as I will probably never again be given the opportunity to resolve the differences between them and their daughter.

The one other thing that Shirley asked me was if I could make sure, on her return to spirit, that her parents would not come for her. The pain I felt from Shirley was so strong and so deep that for the first time I was at a loss for words. Her parents could hear what she was saying during the session. They were holding hands as they looked at Shirley and then they walked into the distance and I could see no farther. They finally accepted their daughter's wishes and, even though Shirley has been for appointments since, they have never returned to offer any advice or help and Shirley is very happy about that.

Lucy

Another client, Lucy, came for a session and I could clearly see that she had been abused by her late father. But Lucy, unlike Shirley, was open to forgiving her parent.

I opened the reading up so that she could ask him directly why he'd done what he had to her. Her father responded that he had been very ill and, at that time, he didn't really know why he'd treated her the way he had. When he realized the devastation he'd brought to both her and the family, he took his own life.

Lucy listened carefully and her response to her father was that she did forgive him but she also wanted him to know that he had caused great pain as she had found out that he had also been abusive to another sister. The downward spiral of events had made Lucy's mother very ill and she was now receiving counseling for some serious mental health issues.

As Lucy was leaving I gave her a hug from her father and she responded by saying, "Even though my father did what he did to me, I now have a family of my own and I will try and let them live their own lives, but I am so protective of them. I hope that I can be strong enough to put this behind me now."

Lucy has been in touch since that time and she seems to be doing okay.

Ben

I always try to place myself in my client's position as to the hurt and pain they are feeling over the loss of a loved one, but when I have to deal with the passing of a child, I do find it extremely difficult to put my emotions aside.

One such reading that occurred about four years ago dealt with the tragic passing of Ben, who had been nearly five when he passed over from choking on something he had swallowed while being held in his mother's arms. There was nothing the mother could do as she could not dislodge the object from his throat.

This is one reading I will never forget and the pain for his mother and for me is still as raw as on the day that Ben passed. All his mum could say to me was, "Tell him I'm sorry, as I feel that I wasn't a good mother in not being able to protect him from danger."

I said, "There are no explanations for why these things happen."

She replied, "I do not believe that there is a God—why would he allow this to happen to my baby?"

I told her that I understood why she would feel that way but if she didn't believe then there might not be a way to make contact with Ben. I truly emphasized and sympathized and wished her to believe that she would reunite with her son one day in heaven. I also told her that Ben visited both her and his dad regularly.

She told me that she continued to sleep with Ben's pillow because it still had his scent on it.

When Ben came through, I noticed that his hair coloring was so different from that of his other siblings and I commented on that to his mother. They all had dark hair and his hair was blonde. Whenever I see this with a child—when the physical appearance is radically different from those of the other children in the home—I believe that the child was an angel on loan for a short period of time.

Ben's mother went away totally at ease with what had been said and she told me before she left that she was happy that she had met me and we both hugged and cried together.

It was debatable who was comforting whom.

⌒

The session with Ben's mother took me back to my nursing days when I had seen another case of a young boy who choked on a tiny superball. It had happened on Christmas Eve of 1988 and we kept him on a life support machine until December 27.

I thought that I had come to terms with that incident, but it was quite obvious that I hadn't as I was feeling the same pain again after the reading for Ben's mother.

My mother, father, and family from the spirit world came to comfort me about what I had had to deal with on the day of the Ben reading. If I had had other appointments that day I would not have been able to fulfill them as the tragic loss of that child had felt like one of my own. It made me question why I don't feel I am ever strong enough in these circumstances. Dad, in that lovely, soothing, and reassuring voice said, "That's why you're special, Bridget, and why people come to you from all over the world."

I felt a peace settle over me and gave myself a hug, believing that it was really Dad who was holding me.

Then I wondered what tomorrow would bring.

Charlotte

One of the clients who sticks in my mind is a young woman named Charlotte who came to see me in 1997. The reading was a four-year one and throughout it I had seen quite serious gynecological problems, which I felt would need to be investigated further. When I told Charlotte about what I had seen she listened intently to what I had to say. After this the situation was in her hands as to whether or not she would continue forward and seek advice from a physician.

About two years later, in 1999, Charlotte started experiencing problems. When she consulted with her doctor she was diagnosed with irritable bowel syndrome (IBS) and told that her symptoms were consistent with the condition.

As time passed Charlotte visited me regularly for readings as there were lots of different things happening in her life—but the health issue that I had initially seen in her reading in 1997 kept coming up. I could foresee continued worsening of problems with her reproductive organs. I could also see that she would go on to change her career and become a mother to a little girl—but I was very worried at the outcome of the pregnancy due to what I had seen.

In 2001, when Charlotte visited a beautician, she was told that her skin was not healthy and that this was almost certainly due to gynecological problems. Charlotte visited her doctor once again and was then referred to a consultant. When the consultant went back and checked the notes on Charlotte from 1995, when she had been a fifteen-year-old, it was found that she had, at that point in time, been feeling very ill and had pain down the right-hand side of her body. At that time the doctor thought she was either pregnant or had something going on with her appendix.

Time went by and I assumed that everything had been sorted out with Charlotte until one day in 2010 when Kenn and I went to a new coffee shop in Halifax—a place that had once been the Halifax Registry Office. As we were waiting for our coffees, my attention was drawn to a voice I recognized and I turned to see who it was. There were Charlotte and her mum, Andrea, also having coffee. I went over to see them and found out that Charlotte was six months pregnant with a baby girl.

But I found that there would be a price to pay for this birth as a scan had found an abdominal mass and decisions would have to be made about the pregnancy. My gut feeling was that Charlotte should go ahead with the pregnancy as I saw that it was the only chance she would ever have of becoming a mother.

After this Charlotte's mum visited me for a reading and it was mentioned in the reading that there was a concern over Charlotte getting blood clots in her lungs.

Charlotte wanted to tell her story about the events as they occurred. Here is her story in her own words:

"Yes, I went to see Bridget for several readings and she was spot-on with what she saw. My health problems had begun when I was a teenager. The doctors I had been to had prescribed anti-inflammatory medications but this didn't happen until 2003. It was clear to me that the real health issues I was having were not being targeted. I was eventually told I had what was known as a 'grumbling appendix,' and I was later to find that this term was not even real because it is a diagnosis doctors give when they have no idea what is wrong with a patient.

"My pain and sickness kept coming and going, sometimes months apart. Visits to the doctors gave no help. I kept getting told that I had IBS, pelvic inflammatory disorder, or ovulation pains. A colonoscopy was performed with no results and I was discharged. My skin was going through noticeable changes and the outbreaks would sometimes be very bad so I booked a facial to try and control this. The beautician used to be a nurse and she said that the condition of my skin was really symptomatic of a gynecological problem. She advised that I go back to my doctor and demand to be referred to a gynecologist. I did this but things didn't go down well with my general practitioner. I believe they felt I was overriding the diagnosis I had been given and in effect I was doing just that. I knew my own body and I knew that something wasn't right with it. I saw the gynecologist and he performed a laparoscopy as he suspected endometriosis. The results were clear of this but he did say that there was scar tissue on my right fallopian tube, and I would probably struggle to conceive. This news devastated me, yet I still had no firm diagnosis as to what exactly was causing my symptoms and now I was also burdened with the worry of not knowing if I could have a child—something that I had always wanted.

"Problems continued and by 2008 I had my second laparoscopy as I was now getting pains around my liver and there was concern that I might have developed scar tissue in that area. Again the test proved clear. I can't begin to tell you how frustrated I was becoming by this time. I didn't want anything negative found, yet I needed answers to my questions about what was happening to my body. This had been going on now for ten years with no definitive diagnosis and my symptoms were worsening.

"In 2008 my husband and I decided we were both ready to start trying for a baby, knowing that there could be problems and even the possibility of having assisted conception. But we decided to go ahead sooner rather than later.

"By March 2009 we had been trying to conceive for eight months with nothing happening except now I was getting pelvic pain with backache. I was at that time in the midst of doing my nurse training. Things were so uncomfortable for me physically that I decided to go back to the doctors. I was dreading it as they made me feel like I was a nuisance and imagining these symptoms. The doctor again wasn't impressed and said, 'You do realize you've taken an urgent or emergency appointment to discuss this?'"

"I told this doctor that it was urgent to me as I was getting more and more symptoms. She told me it was indigestion and prescribed another medication. I couldn't believe it. They just weren't taking me seriously.

"By May I had developed some spotting but ignored it as I didn't want to return to the doctors. My menstrual cycle followed a week later. In June I began to feel really sickly but a different type of sickness. I did a pregnancy test and it was positive. My husband and I were so happy. A couple of weeks later I was really struggling with the backache. I went to have a scan done. To my horror it was found that a large mass had been discovered and there was grave concern about it. I wasn't allowed to leave until I had seen a gynecologist. I pleaded with them to allow me to return to my own gynecologist because they were aware of my ongoing problems. At an appointment with the MD I was reassured that this mass couldn't be anything sinister.

"I was six weeks pregnant at this time and I was told by the gynecologist that I would be left until the twenty-week scan as they don't do anything unless the mass exceeded 10 cm.

"The twenty-week scan revealed the mass had doubled and exceeded 12 cm. They referred me for another immediate gynecological appointment. This doctor decided that I needed surgery and the mass removed along with my right ovary and fallopian tube. I was twenty-two weeks pregnant at the time of my surgery. The histology results came back as a borderline tumor and as a formality the oncologist wanted a CT scan done six weeks after I'd given birth so that the staging could be completed.

"Taking Bridget's advice, I continued with my pregnancy and gave birth to our daughter, Isabella.

"When it came time for my appointment with the oncologist my husband, James, our daughter Isabella, and my mum went with me to the appointment. In the waiting room I knew that something was wrong as the consultant would not make eye contact with me. When we all moved into the consultation room, he began by asking me how my appetite had been. He told me he was really sorry but that 'it' had spread and it was now in the left ovary and liver and it was labeled as stage-three ovarian cancer.

"I couldn't take this in and kept asking what had spread. I yelled out, 'You're not telling me I have cancer!'

"The gynecologist told me he was afraid I was right and then he proposed treatment. This would be a total hysterectomy. He also gave me the option of keeping my uterus if I wanted to go down that path and have an egg donor one day but I wanted him to take everything. All I wanted was to see Isabella grow up—another baby wasn't an issue. Isabella was everything but now my worst fear was that she was going to be left without her mummy.

"Surgery went ahead and my consultant came to me and told me that since my appendix looked abnormal they had gone ahead and removed it. Three weeks after my surgery, the histology results came back and we returned to the clinic to get the results.

"It was good news!

"It wasn't ovarian cancer but in fact it had been cancer of the appendix. It was low grade and the prognosis was good. There are only two centers in this country that treat this as it so rare—1 in 1.7 million—and I was referred to one of these. I would have to go once every six months to be monitored at The Christie in Manchester. I was to have scans. I would eventually require more surgery and then would go on to enjoy much improved health.

"Everything Bridget had seen had come to pass."

~

Throughout the readings I have done there is a continuous running of themes such as love, forgiveness, and acceptance, and this is true for those on both sides of life's doorway. At times the sadness and regret of a damaged relationship carries over into the spirit world and regret tinges the heart and soul of the one that has passed as much as it does those left here on earth.

Sometimes the way to healing is through simply saying "I'm sorry" to someone we have differences with—and often those two words are the most difficult to say aloud. But the idea is, I truly believe, to leave this world with as few regrets as possible so that we go to our new life in spirit free of emotional burdens. And if those of us left here could try our best to release old resentments, then we would be well prepared for our own journeys to spirit one day.

As the sessions presented here and the ones to come point out, there is most definitely an unbroken link between us and our departed loved ones, and it is so much nicer when the link is one of love.

CHAPTER 5
A Few Skeptics

Over the years since I began doing readings and public speaking about my gifts, I have encountered a few people who were very skeptical about what I could do—and this is only natural.

I always do my best to reassure people and offer valid proofs to all, often through specific messages I receive from spirits who kindly give me validation that they are indeed who they say they are.

One of these special sessions was with a lady named Anne.

Anne's husband had passed away suddenly while she was at work. She explained that a week or so before he passed, they hadn't been on very good speaking terms and that was the memory that she had been holding onto.

When she came through my door I could clearly see her late husband was with her. He immediately told me his name and the first thing he said to me was, "Please tell her, Bridget, that all our disagreements have been forgotten and I love her just as much today as I did when I first met her. My passing was very sudden, with a heart attack, but every day I do come to visit her and although we might not always have seen eye to eye, the fact of the matter is that if I had to choose my life and wife over again, I would still have chosen Anne."

I watched Anne's face closely as I told her what her husband had said and I could see that it was all making sense to her, but at the same time I could feel the pain in her heart and the sadness etched on her face. It was obvious to me that if she could turn back the hands of time she surely would.

Anne has been to see me three times in the last two years and, although no reading has been the same, the one thing that remains unchanged is the love that her husband sends to her. A bit of a skeptic, Anne told me that she had sent a message out to her husband beforehand. She told me that she "believed 99.9 percent" in my work, and the communication between the spirit world—but if I could confirm to her what only she and her husband would know, then she would "believe 100 percent."

I am not often put on the spot in this way, but at the same time, I believed that if there was something that her husband wanted to say to validate this, then he would say it. Within seconds he said, "Tell her that I never really liked her smoking anyway and I was with her when she decided to have a cigarette in the bedroom and she knew I was there."

The look on Anne's face and the scream that subsequently followed told me that her question had been answered and that now she could walk away from my office knowing that all of the sadness she had endured over the last few years was finally put to rest.

She promised her husband that she would never smoke again.

$\backsim$

Richard called into the office to make an appointment for his wife. He told Julie and me that he wasn't entirely sure that he believed in my work but his wife wanted a reading with me and he was more than happy to arrange this for her.

Kathryn came for her appointment and, during the reading, Richard's father who had passed to spirit came through and told me that Richard had his watch. Kathryn said she could not confirm that that was true, but she would certainly ask Richard when she got home.

During Kathryn's reading I could also see what would have been the loss of their first child and that it had been a boy. Kathryn became very emotional when I told her this. I assured her that her child was being looked after by his granddad and other family members in heaven. The name of the child in spirit came to me as Jack. Kathryn said she was amazed as that was the very name that had been chosen for the baby should it have been a boy.

I then confirmed to her that Richard's dad was telling me that she was pregnant again.

She told me that she was not aware that she was pregnant but there was such a lovely smile on her face.

Four days later, I had a lovely surprise when Richard called into the office to confirm that he did have his father's watch and also to tell us that Kathryn was pregnant. In his own words he told Julie and me that he could not believe what had been revealed during the reading. "How did you know so much about my father when you had never met him, and about the watch? He gave me his watch to change the battery and it was still in my possession after his passing. I now know from the reading that the watch has to remain with me. It has given me the opportunity to accept my father's passing and to look forward to the new life that is coming. I want to thank you for reassuring me that, although we lose our loved ones at a time when we are not ready, at least I know that Dad is aware of things that are happening on the earth. I feel so happy!"

The smile on his face told me that everything he had heard in the reading had fit into place and he went away from the office saying, "I will come and see you, as before I wasn't ready for the reading, but now I am."

I wished him well.

It was not only nice to have good news but to know that he had moved from being somewhat skeptical to believing in my gift—a validation given by the reading for his wife.

The reading with Kathryn brings in a detail about the afterlife that many find very comforting: the fact that children, from yet unborn to older, are cared for in heaven by family and friends and they, like our more mature loved ones who pass to spirit, await reunion with us when our time comes to leave the earthly plane.

⌒

When I visit Ireland for appointments I always feel that my gift is put to the test, mainly because of the aforementioned increased passings of young people from unforeseen health conditions or tragic accidents.

But wherever I go, I am often asked by a client if a departed loved one in spirit could give a sign to validate that it is indeed they who are coming through.

Such was the case with a mum who came to me who had lost her son due to a pulmonary embolism. Michael was in his thirties and had a wonderful life traveling as a biker. He had left Ireland to visit the place of his birth in Australia, only to pass suddenly from the embolism.

The shock and despair that this brought to his family—but most especially to his mother, who could not come to accept that she would never see her son again—was heart-wrenching. I reassured her, in the best way I could, of my knowledge of what happens when a person passes at such an early age. Although she was happy with what she heard, I knew in my heart that she wanted to stay with me so that she could continue to experience the link between earth and the spirit world.

Michael's mother came to see me when I returned to Ireland in April of 2012 and the pain on her face seemed to have lifted a bit since our last meeting. Michael came through and it was obvious that though he was understand-ably shocked by his sudden departure, he also wanted to re-assure his mother and his family that he was safe in heaven and with his grandparents from both sides of the family. Michael also wanted his mother to enjoy her life with the other family members she had until the day came when they would be reunited once more. Michael's mother ac-cepted this communication from her son, but seemed to want validation.

She asked me, "Is there any way that Michael can tell me now when he will contact me so I can go away from here feeling at peace?"

Neither Michael's mother nor I will ever forget what happened next.

Just at the moment she asked the question, her mobile phone—which had been placed on the table throughout the course of the reading and that she was certain she had turned off—started ringing.

A bit shocked by the occurrence, she checked the phone. The words "Unknown Server" came up on the screen. When she answered the call there was no one at the other end. She said to me, "I have just had the most wonderful feeling that that was my son."

Then the phone rang again with exactly the same message.

Michael's mom had received the validation that she needed to begin healing.

We both held hands and, for the first time, the pain just left her face. She said, "I promise you I will accept that my son has left me and I now know that when my time comes he will be the one that will return to take me home."

We both hugged and when she got outside she was met by my friend, Noreen, and she started to tell her what had happened. We were all filled with emotion and all knew in our hearts that it had been Michael who had made the contact she had asked for.

❦

For all of us who truly believe and know that there is life after death, there is nothing to fear. When our time comes we will be continuing in our eternal life. I always feel sad when people do not want to believe that eternal life exists and that they will never again see their loved ones. I can only reassure these people that from a very young age I was glad that God chose me out of all of my family to spread the wonderful news that there is no death, just a continuation of life eternal.

CHAPTER 6
Audiences and Appointments

My first audience was in November of 1994, held at the Bedford Street Spiritualist Church in Halifax.

It came about that my friend Linda and I wanted to try a different Spiritualist church rather than my own at Sowerby Bridge.

Linda and I decided to dress casually for the night. The service at the Bedford Street church was scheduled to start at 6:00 p.m. but at 5:15 p.m. that evening one of my spirit guides, Betty, came through and spoke to me: "You had better change out of those jeans and top as you are going to be taking your first platform tonight."

I said, "No. There is a speaker booked. I'm only going to see if anyone has a message for me."

Betty very strongly urged me to change into an outfit suitable for the platform.

When Linda turned up at my house at 5:30 p.m. and I came out dressed up, she said, "What are you doing dressed up when we are supposed to be casual?"

I told her what Betty had said and Linda responded with, "Oh, we will have to wait and see then."

The church was only a short distance away and we got there at 5:45 p.m. The building had seating for only about fifty people and I had never been there before. I couldn't help noticing that the building looked to be in desperate need of repair.

Everyone turned and looked at both of us when we entered the church and I felt this was probably because we were newcomers. Our arrival did cause some whispering among those in the congregation. I heard one lady say to another: "We are in for a good night tonight as she is supposed to be a good medium."

I turned and said to the woman, "Actually, I am not supposed to be on here tonight, but according to spirit I am."

Six p.m. came and the service should have begun, but there was no speaker. By 6:20 p.m. the lady who would normally have introduced the speaker stood and apologized to us. She asked if there was anyone in the congregation who could take the service. Before I had a chance to say anything, Linda informed the woman that spirit had already given me the message that I would be the one to take the service that evening—and that is how it began.

We had a wonderful evening; everyone in the congregation got a message from spirit and the messages were understood by all the recipients. Of course, due to the nature of some of the messages there were lots of tears among those gathered. At the end of my service, which went on for an hour, many of those gathered asked me what my fee would be. I told them that I did not want a fee, but that I would be coming next week as I was hoping to get a message from spirit from the speaker.

Other mediums I have met have questioned me as to why I never charge a fee and I tell them that it is my choice because I feel that using my gift in this way keeps the church filled and that keeps the doors open. There is always a collection in church and I know that sometimes after they pay for a speaker there isn't much left for the church to use itself.

~

Every audience is different, but each one I have held since that first one has several things in common—time and preparation. These two elements are definitely a must as far as communication with the spirit world is concerned and I have to take the time to prepare myself to work with my spirit guides and inspirers prior to the event.

I prepare myself for the audience by meditating and linking with my loved ones in spirit who will be working with me. I ask only for the best and most sound advice to be given to the people in the audience who have come in hopes of receiving messages from their loved ones who have passed.

During the audience I am always guided to the person who needs a message by a light that will shine just above their head. Each light is visible only to me and will have a different color and significance attached to it.

A white light represents a recent passing and, if an angel appears within that light, it means that there has been the loss of a child or a baby. The giving of this message usually causes a great deal of emotion among those present because the news of a child or baby passing is heartbreaking to them. Yet, the message also gives great comfort to the person receiving it because the reassurance is that even though the child didn't stay on earth for long, their birthday continues to be celebrated with them during their heavenly life.

A green light means that the person I am speaking with needs guidance and reassurance that a better time lies ahead for them and that they must believe in themselves in order to move on. This does not mean that the person is about to pass to spirit. Rather, it is a clear indication that there must be belief as well as trust in loved ones who are in spirit.

A blue light lets me know that the person I am interacting with has not been too well and needs to be reassured that healing is on the way to them by means of hands, healing prayer, or the lighting of a candle with prayer done especially for the particular condition they are suffering from.

Seeing a red light above the person's head means that there is definitely a health condition that needs sorting out. For instance, the body is not able to fight against infection or the person is awaiting some kind of surgery or treatment. This can be a difficult subject to talk about in an open audience. What I do is to take the message as far as I can and then tell them that I would like to speak to them in private at the end of the evening. At that point I will determine whether I should tell them what I have seen and give them the opportunity to decide if they should come for a private appointment with me or not.

Purple and lavender lights tell me that the person I am speaking with is already receiving treatment for a particular condition and that the spirit world and the loved ones of this person who have passed over are aware of what is needed.

Yellow or orange lights mean the passing on of messages from loved ones in spirit and also could mean spiritual growth. It could also mean that the person before me has the ability to communicate, firsthand, with loved ones who have transitioned to spirit.

Sometimes spirit will ask for a rose bush or a plant to be placed in their name in the garden of the person I am speaking with. The reason for this is because 90 percent of the people who come through with a message will give a rose to the person I am talking with. When a rose bush is planted and it grows and blooms well, it means that the person who is in spirit has also grown spiritually and has accepted their eternal life. Many will name the plant after the departed one. It also gives great comfort to the ones left behind to know that their loved one has never left them. I always pass this message on but, more often than not, the person has already done the planting. It is nice to know that the connection was made.

The next Sunday Linda and I returned to the church, only to find that the speaker again had not turned up. I realized then that my spirit guides and inspirers thought it was time for me to take the platform. After this second service, the church asked if they could book me for a service later on in the year and I said yes. The word quickly got around about my abilities and many more spiritual churches got in touch with me. Thankfully, that has continued for me from that first night at Bedford Street Spiritualist Church to the present.

I now do audiences at many different venues such as clubs, halls, hotels, and theatres. The theatres, clubs, and hotels host an evening where we can all sit down and enjoy a meal before I give my messages. As far as I am aware, I am the only clairvoyant medium who does that. I think that it is lovely that we can all sit down together and have a sociable and enjoyable evening with spirit.

I find it very interesting that quite often in my audiences of late there are always two or three people who have the same abilities as myself. I will know this because my guides and inspirers prompt me to go to these people and give them messages. Those messages can even be about spirit encouraging them to open up about their gifts. I always ask the person in the audience why they have attended that evening and most will tell me that they find my messages reassuring. Many ask if I would be interested in teaching them how to open up their mind about spirit.

◯∕◯

Over the years since I decided to become a full-time medium, I have visited many places for appointments and audiences—Scotland, the Channel Islands, and various sites in the U.K.—but somehow I find that Ireland appears to have so many more tragic cases than any other. I've often thought that this may be because it is such a small country and everyone seems to know everyone else. Having been born there myself, I must say that I still have not heard of as much sadness as I do today. There seem to be so many more suicides, freak accidents such as farm catastrophes, and loss of children's lives. One instance I had was when a television had fallen on top of a child and the child had died as a result. Of course, people question why God would let this happen. I tell them that there always seems to be a reason for everything, but I must admit that I find this sort of tragedy very hard to deal with myself.

I often wonder how other mediums deal with these kinds of messages—or is it just me that spirit seems to give more detailed messages to?

Whenever I am in Ireland I visit the graves of my parents and grandparents on a regular basis, but I also try to visit the gravesites of other people as well—mostly those whose loved ones I had given messages to and who have asked me to visit.

People do often ask me if I think that their loved ones would like them to visit their graves and I always say that it is up to the individual—whatever they feel is right for them. I do tend to remind them that it is only the shell of their loved one in the grave and that the spirit is in heaven. Some of the graves I visit are desolate, others are just spectacular with photographs and flowers and this is always very heartening to see.

Every time I return to Ireland for appointments or holidays, I always look forward to meeting with clients I have met before and visiting family and friends.

But a recent visit during the latter part of 2012 was somehow different.

David

The people I met for appointments were very nice and I found I was quite surprised at how many new clients I had. Yet during this time I couldn't help but feel a somewhat deeper sense of loss overshadowing the time we sat together. There was also much questioning about why people seemed to be passing to spirit at such young ages and under tragic circumstances.

One lady who came to see me told me that her son, David, had gone out one night for a drink. Prior to his leaving he had told her that he wouldn't be late coming home—that he would be leaving his car and getting a lift home. There was no reason for her not to believe her son as he was a sensible young man with so much to live for.

At four in the morning there came a knock on the door of the family home and she was informed that David had been involved in a tragic accident. He had gone off the road and hit a wall and he had been alone. His injuries were so severe that there was very little chance of his survival and he passed soon afterward.

I sat and listened to his mum tell me that he was the eldest of six children and her only son.

Times like these put me under immense stress and there is an intense need to take a few moments to answer all the questions that the client has. David's mum said to me, "Don't tell me that there is a God—a God who would take my only son the way he did."

David was speaking to me from spirit and I took a few moments before I responded with the words he had given me to share with her. "It was not God's fault that I have gone, Mum. I had a choice to get a lift home or to think that I was capable to drive home and I chose to do that. I fell asleep at the wheel of my car and I never felt any pain. I just woke up in spirit surrounded by my angels who are healing me now. But God said he understood why you and Dad are feeling the way that you are, but that each one of my five sisters will bring you comfort in my loss."

David's mum then showed me a family group photograph where all eight members of the family were together. David's mum said, "I don't know what made me decide to have one done now and not for Christmas as was planned." I felt her pain so deeply and said, "At least you have all of them happy and together as well as your husband, Tony, and no one can take any of your memories away."

David's mum then went on to share with me that when David was born, a voice in her head had told her that he was lent to her and not given.

As she was speaking, the words kept coming into my head that she was going to have to be strong for her family as they needed her. But the pain I felt within my heart told me that it was going to take a long time for her to accept what had happened and also to accept again the enjoyment of life as she had seen how quickly it could all end.

Rita

Another lady named Rita came to me for a reading during this trip. When she saw me she gave me a big hug and thanked me so much for saving her life. As I see so many people over the course of time, I asked her if I had met with her before and she said, "Yes. I saw you six years ago." She explained that she had come with her daughter and her daughter's friend. She told me that she had been a skeptic and I said, "That's okay. But what has made you come back again if you didn't believe?"

"Well," she said after her reading concluded, "you have done my reading now, so I will tell you. You picked up on scar tissue from my previous surgery and you also said that I was a very lucky lady. When I came to you six years ago my daughter, Haley, went in first to see you while her friend and I sat out in the car. Before Haley went in, I told both girls that I was a nonbeliever and that I had decided not to have the reading with you. You told my daughter that I was sitting out in the car and, even though I had decided not to go through with the reading, that there was something very important that you needed to tell me and that there was no way I could say no."

She continued. "When I came in you made me feel very welcome. You told me that you had a man and a woman, both in spirit, who were telling you that they were my parents and my mum was telling you that I needed major surgery and you pointed to my kidney area. I went on to tell you that I had had pain in that area, but I had seen three different doctors who had all told me that I had to lose weight and that they could find nothing wrong. After I had been to see you, I made an appointment with one of the doctors that I had seen before. I told him that I had been to see you and what you had told me. He told me that I had better lie down on the doctor's table and have an exam. On examination he said to me, 'This is serious. I feel a rather large lump on your right kidney and you need further investigation, so you must attend this appointment in Dublin this week at a hospital that specializes in the kidneys.'"

Rita went on with her story. "So, I went to the appointment in Dublin and was told that I had a malignant tumor in my kidney. I had it removed. Thank God I am still in remission to this day and it is thanks to you, Bridget, that I am still here."

She next asked if it would be okay if she wrote to a magazine to tell them her story as she felt that it could go on to help many other people in the same position that she had been in. I spent some time thanking spirit on her behalf, especially her parents, who had insisted that she go to the doctors and have an examination.

Katie

I do find that my gift is unique in many ways, but sometimes it is hard to have to tell someone that their loved ones are leaving this earth. This happened to my cousin's mum, Katie Knight. She was the last one of my mum's generation here on earth and while I was in Ireland this time, Katie was admitted to hospital with breathing difficulties. When I went to see her on October 21, 2012, she looked weak and tired. I was there with her daughter, Mary, and my friend, Noreen. Katie managed to have a conversation with me and I was able to tell her about our son Mathew's marriage to Rachel. Also, I told her all about Kenny, our second grandson, who was born on July 4, 2012. I shared with her that my family sent their best wishes to her. When I asked her how she was feeling she didn't reply, although her eyes told me that she had had enough; she appeared quite exhausted and I thought she was most likely very much looking forward to joining her husband, John, who had passed to spirit nearly two years before on November 2, 2010. I felt that Katie would join him just before that date.

On October 22, Katie slipped into a coma and remained that way until she passed to spirit on the 29th. She was buried on November 2, the second-year anniversary of her husband's death.

I would miss Katie very much as she always had a great story of the past to tell, but I was also relieved that she was now out of her pain.

As it always does when a family member passes to spirit, life will change in Katie's home, especially for her daughter, Mary, who took care of all her mum's needs on a 24/7 basis. There are other family members but it was always Mary that Katie knew would never fail to be at the hospital every day. She never missed once and always made sure that her mum got the very best of care. Mary had also been her dad's caregiver with the same routine. In two years all that has changed. It is my sincere hope that Mary will now be able to enjoy her life by being able to visit her son, John, his wife, Lorri, and her beautiful granddaughter who live in Boston, in the United States.

If anyone deserves a gold medal for hard work, dedication, and patience, it surely is Mary.

Trying to Understand Why

Many people who visited me for appointments while I was in Ireland had different stories and views to share as far as spirit was concerned, but every day there was a different tragedy to deal with.

One young man took his two daughters—one aged about two and the other aged three or four months—out for a walk while his wife was making dinner at about 12:30 p.m. on Sunday, October 28, 2012. A car suddenly careered out of control, hit the children, and killed them. The driver, a young man, had had a seizure while driving. The father and the driver survived.

I was asked why such a horrible thing had happened and I have to admit I sometimes don't have the answers. I tried to reassure people that heaven now has two more little angels, but at the same time I often question the timing of such events myself.

The answer that came back from spirit was that they were in the wrong place at the wrong time. It seemed not a good enough answer, but it was the only one received.

I knew that the driver of the car would not have been able to prevent such a thing from happening, but at least the news that the driver hadn't been drinking or speeding reassured the public to a degree.

It is my sincerest hope that God and spirit give both parties the strength to accept the things that cannot be changed, to change the things they can, and the wisdom to know the difference.

The most comforting thing about an audience is that other people who may be skeptical hear the messages that I am giving.

I remember clearly an audience I gave in Ireland in October, 2011. That audience was a tearjerker from the beginning to the end. Each message had a deeper meaning to it. One lady that I came to had lost her little boy, John, at the age of three when he climbed into a slurry pit on the farm and lost his life. She was at work and the news had to be broken to her by her husband. Now she had just lost a second son with what was thought to be cancer because it involved his liver, but in actual fact, alcohol was the cause of death. My telling her about her little three-year old son took her right back to that day and she kept asking me where I was getting the information from. I told her it was from her late parents. Although she was very distraught, she seemed comforted by the fact that her family were united in the spirit world and contact was made.

There were gasps of amazement tinged with sadness.

Keiron

Another lady in that same audience had lost her fifteen-year-old son to hanging. She had traveled from another county to try and make contact with his spirit. In front of all those present she told me that she had been to several other spiritual evenings only to have her son, Keiron, come through and tell her that he had waited for the time that he could make contact with me as I was Irish.

Keiron explained to his mum that there was no reason within his family for him to take his own life, only that he hadn't been happy with this world, but he had found peace and tranquility in his new home in heaven. In heaven he said he had become a great inspirer and willing participant in helping other children who had left this world much younger than he had been.

His mum was so distraught and told me she couldn't go on living without him. I spent a lot of time with her afterward—she promised me that she would come to see me in person and an appointment was made for her. I later found that she had taken her own life three days after my message from her son. In hindsight and deep down, I knew that I would never see her again. I felt honored and privileged that Keiron had reassured his mum through me that he was safe, but I also felt so sad that she went to such lengths to be able to join him.

I have had a message from her since she went to the spirit world. She thanked me and asked me to forgive her, but Keiron was her only child and she just couldn't go on living without him.

They are now resting in peace, together forever.

At the end of that evening I felt totally drained on every level after giving fifty-five messages, most of which were tragic. I suddenly felt the presence of my mother and father. They came side by side and said to me, "You know that we are always with you, Bridget, and to make you laugh, can you just ask that last man that you delivered a message to about his parents to stand up?"

I did, and both of them said to me, "That man is now the owner of the land where you used to make the cocks of hay and play with your spirit friends and fairies." When asked, the man agreed that he had bought the land but he wasn't the man that Mum first sold it to. He had bought it off the previous owner and he told me that if I ever wanted to visit that field, I was more than welcome.

I haven't done that yet, but I will.

Jake

As the years went on I dealt with a family whose first son, Jake had been born on December 21, 1993. He came into the world with a condition called "Inside Out." This is a condition where the baby's abdomen is open and all the intestines are exposed in the mum's womb. Jake was taken to surgery immediately after birth, but went back to spirit on December 17, 1994. I had seen this baby coming into the world and also going out of it.

I will never forget the day of Jake's funeral, December 24. It was a cold and frosty day and the church was packed.

I went to say goodbye to Jake before they closed the coffin. It was so painful as my youngest son, Marcus, was just two years of age at the time.

It was also very hard because all the hymns that were sung were Christmas songs and everyone sang as loud as they possibly could the hymn "Away in a Manger." All I could think of was that it should have been a special hymn as it represented Jesus being born, and yet, here we were handing Jake back to spirit—a child that had only been on loan.

When we got to the gravesite and his coffin was being lowered into the ground, the anguish and pain on both the parents' faces will remain with me forever. And, even though they were no longer together as a couple, I held the mum's hand and said to her, "There is a little girl coming and it is Jake's sister." She looked at me in shock, but nine months later his little sister came into the world and it brought such happiness to all of us. It was as if spirit was telling me that there can only be one Jake, but because of his sister's birth he will live on forever.

Jake's mother told me that she and Jake's dad had gotten back together briefly. The baby that resulted was perfect.

The couple have now gone their separate ways and each have new partners and other children. Even though I do not see them, I will never forget Jake, who, it should be noted, passed to spirit on December 17, the same date that my late father, Charles, passed. It often makes me wonder why certain dates recur.

Jake's family was still devastated so, in order to try and ease their pain in some way, I agreed to do an audience at the Victoria Theatre in Halifax to raise funds for St. James' Hospital in Leeds, where Jake was treated. The Victoria Theatre is large enough to hold a great many people.

The audience took place in November 1995 to a full house. It was an extremely emotional evening, and Jake's mum and grandma were present.

I could not believe how many people turned out to meet me and after the audience was over they came up onto the stage where I gave them each a flower.

My local bank decided to match whatever proceeds I raised that night so we were able to hand over £1,000 once the theatre costs had been deducted.

I decided to do another fundraising event the following year at the same venue, and it was just as successful as the first one.

I do believe that Jake would have lived on anyway and even though I am no longer in touch with his family, his birth and passing will always stay with me—especially his passing—as it was on the same day as the passing of my own dad.

Although I have not received many messages from Jake, the ones I have received are ones in which he lets me know that he does visit his mum and sister.

∞

It can be very difficult when I am working in front of an audience and I am given news of a forthcoming tragedy. I have to think very carefully before giving the message because of its sensitivity. I always ask the person who the communication is for, and if I am allowed to say everything that I am being told. If they say yes, then I go ahead with the whole message. Otherwise, if the entire message cannot be conveyed at the time it is being given to me, the person in spirit may return or not come again.

Although there is a lot of sadness at times within the audience, there is also laughter. For example, one man who came through from spirit with a message was playing hell with me for keeping him waiting a while before his message was delivered to his loved one. He told me that if I didn't hurry up he wasn't going to hang around, even though his loved one was sitting at the opposite side of the room from where I was. When I finally got a chance to give the message, his loved one said, "He hasn't changed then. That's exactly how he was when he was here on earth. He never liked waiting for anything or anyone."

My most recent comical moment was when I had a woman come through who had suffered with a lot of flatulence (or wind) while on earth and that was how she made herself known to me. Her name was Hannah. I found myself burping and had to ask her to control any feeling of flatulence so that she didn't pass this condition on to me! The person in the audience whom the message was for instantly recognized that it was her mother. Bless her, she was roaring with laughter and tears were streaming down her face as she realized her mum still suffered with this condition in spirit!

I reassured her that her mum had only brought this feeling through so that she would be recognized.

⌒〜⌒

During an audience the anticipation level is usually very high as those present wonder and wait to find out if a loved one will come through. And if a painful message has to be delivered, I have been reassured by spirit since I was in my mid-teens that they will be there to help and guide me through.

So Many Questions

During a trip to Ireland, I saw a lady who had lost her husband to a heart attack that happened almost in front of her eyes.

Her husband had complained of indigestion a couple of days before but he had no other symptoms to make her think that it was serious. They had been out shopping and after they had arrived home he described a feeling of "trapped wind" in his chest. She went to get him a drink from the kitchen, and suddenly she heard a loud thud only to come back into the room and find the man she had met and loved since she was sixteen was dead on the floor.

I reassured her during the reading that her husband was in heaven and she looked at me with so much sadness etched on her face and asked, "He is in heaven?"

I was taken aback as to why she should ask this.

I said, "Why? Where do you think he is?"

She replied that she didn't know and then she asked me "Where is heaven?"

I told her that heaven is all around us and the only way that I could describe it to her was as if her husband had immigrated to another island where he was now building a home for her when it was her time to join him.

She then said, "How do I know when he is around?"

I explained that every time he entered her mind and every day and night that she picked up his photograph to speak to him she surely must know that he is with her.

She told me that her heart was broken and that two years on, it still had not mended. I went on to explain how he knew about their new grandson who had recently come into the world and was named after him. The child was trying to help with all the sadness the family had endured and was doing his best to support all of them.

She asked me if her husband would continue to age in spirit as she would on earth and I said, "Yes."

Her husband had met her parents and his own parents and he had recognized them as the people who had come to accompany him on his journey back to spirit. He told me to tell his wife that he would never leave her. It was his heart that had let him down. I could feel her pain and her eyes showed me the sadness that losing her husband had caused. She gave me a hug and to my surprise said, "You have had a lot of sadness too and I want to ask you: how did you accept the loss of loved ones who are supporting you today?"

I paused and said, "When I was given my gift from a very young age, I knew God thought that I was strong enough to accept the things I cannot change, that I had the courage to change the things I could, and the wisdom to know the difference."

We hugged again and I knew that she was leaving with the knowledge and reassurance that one day she would be reunited with her husband.

"One last question before I leave," she said. "Will I die of cancer?"

I asked her why she had asked me this as I had not seen that in her reading and she said, "It was a thought that crossed my mind."

Nothing more was said.

It was comforting to me that she had picked up and recognized the losses that I had had in my life, but it didn't end there.

The very next evening I had a text message on my work phone from a young lady who had been to see me that day and whom I had found had the gift herself. She was overwhelmed that I encouraged her to develop it further. Before she came and after she left, I commented to my friend Noreen that I would hear from this young lady again and yet I couldn't, at that time, think why this might happen. I called the young lady back as I needed to know what it was that she wanted to tell me. She said that in reading my first book, *When Tomorrow Speaks to Me*, she clearly heard my brother, Charles, telling her that I needed protection in my work and that he would be the one who would be there for me. I smiled as I was talking to her and said, "Strangely enough, I had just been thinking about him and that I hadn't heard from him in a while." Then I asked her, "What did he mean by protection?"

She just said that people would expect a lot from me and that I needed to be able to separate myself from my work and my private life.

I understood exactly what she was saying and I thanked her for the message.

It is so true. Sometimes I find that the sadness of the day can stay with me well into the night, which often causes me to be restless. But then I receive a message like this and I am reassured that our loved ones in spirit find many ways to get through to us and let us know that they are still with us and still thinking about our well-being—and the ways that they get in touch can be many and varied. Messages from spirit can often be transmitted to us in both amazing and yet subtle ways. It may be through someone else but it could just as easily be through hearing a particular song being played, a book that had great meaning to the spirit falling from a shelf, or a scent that comes unexpectedly that is reminiscent of the one that has passed on. One just has to be, as I have said, open to receiving the messages that are given.

$$\sim$$

Loved ones from spirit can find a myriad of ways to communicate with us. Some visit in person or form, others through the mind in dreams and thoughts. Sometimes communication happens in rather interesting ways. such as when a well-loved and familiar song plays on the radio, or through a medium like myself. They show themselves to me and I see them as they looked when they passed to spirit. They always explain to me who they are.

When there are tragic accidents or suicides, this is shown to me also by spirit. If a person took their own life, the method that they used will be shown to me by spirit. I will also see the person as they look in the present and after they have fully healed. The person who has recently passed over will not show themselves to a loved one until they have fully healed.

When a person sits down in front of me for a private reading, I only deal with the loved one or ones that come through for that reading. However, when I am holding an audience, it is very different as I have many spirits coming around at the same time and vying for attention. During these readings I rely on spirit to guide me to the person I need to be with.

I also rely on the spirits of my loved ones to prepare me for the day ahead. Usually this is how I find out if the day is going to be a good one or not. For instance, during my most recent trip to Ireland in the spring of 2013, I woke up one morning and was told by my mum that the day would be a difficult one emotionally, but that she would be there to protect and reassure me so that I would be able to deal with whatever was put in front of me—and I was to find out that Mum certainly was right.

Ireland Trip Spring 2013

All of the appointments on this one particular day my mum had cautioned me about were surrounded by tragedy of one kind or another—and then quite suddenly I found myself confronting a situation I had never encountered before.

A couple came for a reading and the woman decided that she wouldn't have hers done as it would be more suited to her partner. When he got out of the car and approached me I had an overwhelming feeling of sadness and felt that no matter what I would say to him, I would not be able to control what lay ahead of him.

The man sat down at my table and the first thing he said to me was, "I do not want this reading recorded."

I explained to him that a recording was part of the appointment fee and he said, "I know, but this time I do not want you to record it."

I asked him if there was a specific reason for this request, but I did not really need an answer from him as I already knew—I just wanted and needed to hear from him that he was going to take his own life. As he did not respond, I began the reading.

A few minutes later he stopped me and told me that there was only one answer he needed to hear and that when it was given he would let me know. Both of his parents came in spirit and I told him that his mother said she would be waiting for him on the other side.

"Thank you very much," he said. "That was all I needed to hear." He paused for a moment then asked, "Is she definitely waiting for me?"

"Yes she is," I said, "but she is also telling me to tell you not to do what you intend to do." I paused and then asked him straight out if he did intend to take his own life because that was the feeling that his mother was giving me. In response he put his head down and said, "When my mum died, part of my heart went with her. I had the best parents that I could have wished for but there is nothing left in this life for me anymore."

The man also told me that he had had an appointment with me four years earlier, when the pending death of his mother had come up in the reading. He said that his mum had passed away a little over a month from the date of that reading. He further stated that I had told him that he would one day be the father to two children—a boy and a girl. When he had left the appointment, he said he thought that would never happen for him but on this day, when he was visiting me, his daughter was in the car and his son's birth was expected in about six weeks.

I truly felt his pain and I asked him if there was anything at all that I could do for him to delay what lay ahead of him—but he did not respond. As I was asking him this, I was also coming to the realization that I could not prevent what was fated for him—the situation was not within my control. I also knew that his partner, who was waiting for him, would be wondering why I hadn't recorded the reading and I expressed this aloud. "Leave that up to me," he said.

When he began to pay me I told him that I couldn't take the money for the reading, but he insisted and said, "You are a very nice lady and we have jerked you about as you were expecting to be doing two readings. I want you to accept this money. There are many people out there who need your help and one of them could have been here if you had known that there was only one appointment."

As he was getting ready to leave he shook my hand and said, "You will never know how happy you have made me feel today." I took the opportunity to remind him that there would be two beautiful children who one day would ask what had happened to their father. He said, "I will be looking down on them and they will understand."

After he left I was so grateful that I didn't have another reading for an hour. For the first time ever, I was at a loss for words because I had just faced somebody who I knew in my heart meant everything he had said and no matter how spiritual and believing I was, there was nothing I could do.

His partner came to the door and asked me if everything was okay and I simply said, "He needs help desperately." I didn't have the heart to tell her what he was going to do as she was carrying his unborn son and I didn't want the news of her partner's plan to in any way affect her or the child. She looked at me as if she divined what was ahead and said quite simply, "I understand."

As I watched them get into their car and drive away, all I could think of was asking God to help them.

Although I feel that I am prepared for any obstacle that is put in my way, I often wonder if I have been chosen to deal with all the tragedies of life. The only thing that I can say is that I was very honest with the man and he certainly was very honest with me. I knew that there was no way I could have ever changed his mind. As it stands, there is only me and him and his mother in spirit who knows everything that was said that day. He knew how I felt but then he ended up reassuring me that what he was going to do was for the best.

I will never forget the sadness in his eyes, even though he gave me such a lovely smile—but there was nothing more to say.

◦⁄◦

Another incident that happened while I was in Ireland this trip occurred when my friend and I were out for a drive. It was a cold, wet, and blustery day, near evening, and we had just passed what is normally a beautiful beach that can be seen from the road.

We slowed the car and I noticed a man who appeared to be wearing only his underpants. He had quite obviously already been in the sea and had recently come out. I looked but could not see any other clothes lying about and it crossed my mind that perhaps I was seeing a spirit who was preparing me for something dire that I would have to face during the coming week. To check whether or not I was seeing a spirit I asked my friend if she could see the man and she said that she could.

Because I felt he needed help I tapped the horn, and he just turned and waved and walked back into the sea as if to say that we had disturbed what he was about to do. And then he just vanished.

I do not know the outcome of this incident as there are so many missing people in Ireland at this time. It is hard to know if he is one of them, but I have no doubt that on my next visit there will be a message for me about this.

Although most of my readings are sad, they make me realize how very grateful I am to have a lovely family that I am able to enjoy when I get a chance to put aside the events of the week and spirit allows me to take some time out as well. As I have gotten older I am able to accept the work that spirit wants me to do more easily because I know that my role is to help and give comfort wherever it is needed. If ever anything wants to linger with me after a full week of appointments, I have to set it free and this I do by visualizing a color of the rainbow and using that color to cleanse my body and soul and bring me peace.

A Very Special Dream

Dreams are a very powerful means by which spirit communicates with us while we are in physical form. This most incredibly vivid dream came to me while I was still in Ireland in the spring of 2013.

In the dream I was taken back to my childhood and the field that we used to make the haycocks on when I was six or seven. Yet in this dream I was my present age and with me were my friend Noreen and my husband, Kenn. Spirit asked me to attend a party in the field and when we all got there I could see teepees and the number six—which I understand to mean conscious compassion necessary for spiritual enlightenment and forgiveness. We were all asked to enter this one particular teepee but I felt that maybe we were too tall, so Noreen and I got on our knees and climbed inside, all the while laughing at what we were doing. Kenn declined to come inside as he said that he was too tall so he waited outside for us. When we got inside there were seven red chairs and sitting on each one was a little man. Two of the men made themselves known to us by the names of Tweedledee and Tweedledum. I had to sit on Tweedledee's chair and Noreen had to sit on Tweedledum's. Tweedledee said to me, "We have called you here today to show you your life's destiny." He then got out a globe of the world and with a cane he pointed to America, Tasmania in Australia, and Canada—then he said, "These are just some of the places that you will visit so that you can help people in other countries to realize that there is another life after death." He then told me that there was an envelope underneath my chair that I was to open. I did as he instructed and found a note that read "Bridget Benson £107,000." He told me that there was £1,000 from each of the men (£7,000 in total) and the rest would come from another source. Then he brought forward a young man who has been working with me from spirit. The young man was Irish and he lost his life in an accident when he was just over six years of age (he would be fifty now) and we were formally introduced. The young man and I had a very long talk and he told me that my books were of interest and that one day I would know of a film where both books would be combined together. He then formed a campfire and everyone—the spirit children, fairies, and leprechauns—came out dancing. I was absolutely amazed that this vision had once more come back to me. Noreen and I were also given a drink of what looked like green herbal tea. I have to say that it didn't taste very good and I commented on this and was told that "it was not the taste that mattered, it was the goodness within it that counted."

The ringing of my phone woke me from the dream. But even though reality intruded, I felt in my heart that the dream had been very real and after the week I had just had, it gave me something to focus on.

We will wait and see what happens!

Afterword

Over the course of the years and because of the work I do, many people have asked me if I have ever given any thought to my own passing to spirit.

It is a question I answer with ease because I have already made a journey to the spirit world.

It was in 1996 that I had to have a hysterectomy. The pain I had been experiencing was unbearable and from my hospital bed I asked for my father and loved ones to come to me from spirit as I badly needed their comfort. Instantly, my father, Charles, and my father-in-law, Cyril, were there with me. And soon after their arrival I left my body behind and found myself flying along beside them.

It didn't seem long before we reached our destination in the spirit world. When we arrived, I was met by a man with shoulder-length white hair and a white beard. He was of medium height and he had the loveliest green eyes. He radiated compassion and understanding. He was dressed in a long, white robe that was decorated with gold. On his head was a cap very similar to that worn by a cardinal or bishop of the Catholic Church. He introduced himself as Saint Peter. My father and father-in-law remained at my side.

I must explain that even though I was raised in a Catholic village in Ireland, I was never made aware of who Saint Peter was as I left the village at a young age after my father died. All of my religious instruction there was always about Jesus and Our Lady. So it was because of our move to England that I had no details about the Apostles as I then attended a non-Catholic school. It wasn't until later that I found out that Saint Peter had been one of Jesus' twelve Apostles and was known as the first pope to the Catholic faith.

The appearance of this kind and caring man who seemed so very concerned about the amount of pain I was in was such a comfort. He seemed to understand without me telling him that I wanted to go to heaven and to stay there where I knew I would be pain-free.

Saint Peter had a ledger in front of him and he asked me my name and I told him I was called Bridget Benson. He looked down at the ledger, which I could plainly see was in alphabetical order, and he said, "We are not expecting you."

I felt a great wave of sadness come over me and said, "Am I expected in another place?"

He said, "No."

He asked me why I had wanted to come and I explained to him that it was because of the pain I was in. He said, "We will take away your pain."

I asked, "Who are *we?*"

"I am just about to show you," he responded. "I will let you come in, but you must return to earth."

"Okay," I said.

Then with both his hands he pushed open what I can only describe as huge wood-paneled doors. To me, standing nearby, it seemed as though there was another force present and helping him open them.

My eyes opened wide with wonder at what I saw before me.

It was a room.

In this room was my husband's grandma, Betty, who appeared to be amazingly young. It was interesting to note that her hair seemed much longer than it had been on earth. I also noticed a little boy next to Betty whom I could not identify. There was also Harry, who had been the first spirit to speak to me when I was three years old. I could also see Great-auntie Bridget, Grandma Kate, and Grand-dad John from my mum's side of the family. There were also many other people there, both young and old, but I didn't recognize any of them until Betty took some time to introduce me to a few of them.

There was no roof on this room or building and I could see only the sun shining down very brightly. Everyone seemed to be busy working at various tasks. Betty was working on a loom. I asked her what she was doing and she told me that she was making woolen blankets that were needed on earth.

Totally amazed, I turned to Dad and Cyril, who had followed me into the room. I asked them what they did here. They took me outside of the room and into a garden full of fresh grown vegetables, trees, and flowers. The perfume of all of these growing things was overwhelming and beautiful.

I asked Dad and Cyril who the little boy was that was with Betty. Cyril told me that this was Daniel, the first grandchild of Hilary, who is Kenn's auntie and Cyril's sister. The child was stillborn on November 19, 1995. As soon as I was made aware of who the child was, I could then plainly see the resemblance to our Andrew, Hilary's son. Daniel had beautiful mousy-brown, tight-curly hair and big green eyes. He was wearing a green striped romper suit (an all-in-one.) He had no shoes on his feet. I was able to pick him up and give him a hug, but even as I did so he smiled at me as if he knew that I did not belong there. I asked Betty why he didn't have on a disposable nappy (diaper) because I had noticed that he was wearing a terry-cloth nappy—the old-fashioned kind. She told me that they did not use disposable nappies in spirit. I also asked her if she took care of Daniel all the time and she told me that she didn't, but that she would show me where he goes when he was not with her. She took me to a nursery that was full of children of the same age and older than Daniel. There were people working in the nursery that didn't seem any different than the nurses on earth who work with infants and children. These nurses were all wearing different colored uniforms, some blue, some green, and some yellow. I noticed that all of the ones dressed in the yellow uniform looked after the babies like Daniel. I was very impressed.

I noted that there were no carpets on the floor of the nursery, just rugs, but not many of them. I questioned Betty about that. She told me that carpets breed germs and that the floor was mopped and cleaned every day with Dettol. I was overwhelmed by all of this and the many similarities to caretaking on earth. I then told Betty that I would let Hilary, Daniel's grandmother, know that he was safe and that he sees his great-grandparents nearly every day.

Suddenly I felt a summons from Saint Peter and returned to a sort of office where he was. He told me that it was time for me to return to earth. I begged and pleaded with him to let me stay and then he asked, "Can I just show you why you need to go back?"

A scene unfolded in front of me and I could see Kenn, Mathew, Elizabeth, and Marcus. I saw that I was lying in a coffin in the dining room of our home and wearing a beautiful black dress. My makeup was perfect. My family was all crying and I knew then I had to return and said aloud to Saint Peter, "I have to go back now."

The next thing I remember was hitting my head on the back of the hospital bed. I opened my eyes to find that I was surrounded by two nurses and a doctor. Kenn had visited me, and because he could not rouse me he had called the nurse and she had alerted the doctor. The first thing my doctor said was, "What happened to you?"

I answered truthfully. "I have just come back from the spirit world."

The doctor looked at me in disbelief but the nurse knew that I was a clairvoyant medium and she told him that she would explain it to him later.

A drip was then placed in my arm. It felt as though I had been away for a long time and I felt that I needed the fluid.

Kenn seemed very upset and asked me if I was going to be all right and I told him that I was. I explained to him that the reason I had come back to him and the family was because it was not yet my time.

I had felt no fear whatsoever during my experience and indeed felt very privileged to have been able to visit the spirit world.

◦◦◦

From the night I had my first communication from Harry at the age of three and all throughout my childhood up to the present day I have never feared death. Thankfully, I have been given enough insight through the years about the spirit world to allow me to share this with people from all over the world.

As I have grown and met so many people from all walks of life, all colors, creeds, and classes, I have found that everyone has their own belief of who their maker (God) is and what sort of destination they expect when they leave this world. I always tell people, as best as I can, about what I have experienced and that the afterlife is where you go when your life work on earth is completed. You take nothing with you but your memories and all pain, sorrow, regrets, and so forth are left behind.

Often I am asked about where the people go who do not make it to heaven. The only answer I can give to that query is that I have only dealt with people who go to heaven, so, therefore, I have no real answer to that question.

I must remark that whenever I have been present with a patient—either in my nursing days or in the present—who is making the transition, I notice that, if they are able, many reach out their arms and I can clearly see the spirit who has come for them. I am able to describe that spirit to relatives and it is always reassuring when they say this is someone they also recognize as either a grandparent, aunt, uncle, mother, father, etc. Sometimes it can be a child who has grown up in the spirit world that comes. In any event, being told that the transitioning loved one is being met and is not taking the journey alone gives great comfort to those left on earth.

Children or anyone who passes who does not have a loved one in the spirit world to come for them during their transition will always be met by angels and those who act as nurses in the afterlife. No one goes alone. There will always be angels covering each corner of the cot or bed. As the old prayer goes:

Matthew, Mark, Luke, and John,
Bless this bed that I lie on.
There are four corners to my bed,
Four angels 'round my head.
One to watch, and one to pray,
And two to bear my soul away.
Now I lay me down to sleep,
I pray the Lord my soul to keep.
If I should die before I wake,
I pray the Lord my soul to take.
If I should die within the hour,
I know he'll take my soul forever.

When I had the amazing opportunity to visit the spirit world, I noticed that there were all kinds of people there but there only seemed to be one person at the front gate to meet me. I asked why this was and I was told that there is something much like shift work and that as people go to the spirit world during all times of the day and night, others take their turn to meet and greet people on their return home.

Thoughts on My Own Passing

I do not speak as often with the children now about my passing as I did when they were younger, but they are all aware of what my wishes are. I truly believe that preparing for this journey home with family and loved ones is a very important thing and should not be overlooked because the subject may be uncomfortable.

I would like my two sons and daughter to carry my coffin if they are able to do that and I would appoint my eldest son, Mathew, to speak on behalf of the family. Elizabeth and Marcus may also speak if they wish to.

Both Kenn and I have now taken on Bethanny, who is seventeen years of age. She is the daughter of Kenn's sister, Lisa, who passed suddenly to spirit on November 25, 2010, at the age of forty-two. I feel that I now have four children and it takes me right back to when I was eighteen and the specialist told me that I would never have any children, and yet my late father said, "You will be the mother of four." I wonder, now, that even though I lost Elisabeth's twin brother, Daniel, was Dad's comment to me at that time meant for now? We love Bethanny with all our hearts and we will make sure that, even though we can never replace her parents, we will always do our best for her. I believe that when a child loses a parent there is always a special gift that we haven't recognized at the time.

The other day I heard Bethanny singing. I closed my eyes and felt I was listening to the singer, Adele, performing "Make You Feel My Love" and "Someone Like You." I asked Bethanny what those songs meant to her. With her eyes welling with tears, she told me they were for her mum and that she had practiced the words over and over until she had got them right. A few months ago she had actually had the courage to sing the songs in front of an audience. I could hear her mum telling me from spirit, "Please find her someone who can help get her voice out there." And that I will do. I know that Lisa will help me find that person who can encourage Bethanny's gift and, if I should pass before Bethanny has met the love of her life, I hope that I will have instilled within her that she should never be scared and never afraid to ask for help.

For my own funeral I will record a CD that I wish to have played, the contents of which will remain private until that day. To each one of my children and grandchildren, I will be leaving a personal CD. For my husband, Kenn, there will be a personal CD as well. I will also include a message for Marcus's father, Ron, as he was also a part of my life.

I would want there to be a big celebration of my life. I do not want anyone to be sad, but I would want them to sing as loudly as they could to the two songs that I have chosen, which are "I Have a Dream" by Abba and "Spirit in the Sky" by Norman Greenbaum. I wish that everyone wear clothing with a color from the rainbow—I do not want any black clothing to be worn.

My greatest wish would be that there would only be family flowers and that there would be a donation box to my favorite charity, the Overgate Hospice in Elland, West

Yorkshire. I have had so many dealings with people with cancer who have now passed over, and with their families. At the time of writing this there are two who have passed and one that is awaiting his transition.

I would like balloons with all the colors of the rainbow released into the sky after the service, which will be totally spiritual and will be held at a venue to accommodate everyone who attends. I know that I am probably asking for a lot, but I feel that the end of my life—as is true for all of us—should be as important as the beginning. Throughout my life I have met and stayed friends with so many people. It is important to me that my life should be celebrated. I do not feel that that time is yet, but when it does come, everyone will know what my wishes are.

༄

It is now Friday, September 28, 2012, and it has been a very emotional day for me as I sit here putting this all down and recalling all the past memories. There is never a day that goes by that I don't think about Mum and Dad, Charlie, Anne, and Johnnie—but today they have remembered me and sent a message from heaven in the form of a beautiful white feather that I found on the floor by the side of my office chair. Julie picked it up and placed it next to Johnnie's photograph and we both said, "Thank you." As there is no other explanation for the feather to be here, I know in my heart that it was delivered from heaven to reassure me that they know how I feel, and even though I have the gift to communicate with those in spirit, it is nice knowing that my loved ones can use this way of letting me know they are nearby and concerned.

I feel so very honored and privileged to be able to work with my loved ones as well as the loved ones of other people. Over the past two years, a very special young Irish man has joined my team of inspirers. He passed to spirit at the age of six and a half years due to an accident and I have become so close with his family. It is like both our families are entwined with so many coincidences such as birthdays, anniversary dates, animals with the same names, and so forth. I feel so blessed that he has chosen to work with me, bringing so much comfort to families of loved ones who have experienced tragic losses. He also continues to bring comfort to his own family because of the messages he sends to them through me.

Mum's Messages

I had been planning a trip to the United States for October 2012, but Mum came to me with a message in the early hours of October 11, which happened to be the thirteenth anniversary of my sister-in-law Steph's passing. Mum told me of the forthcoming devastating effects of a hurricane that was shortly to hit the States and that there would be lives lost as well as many homes. She pointed out that the United States had already had too much to deal with.

So I cancelled all my plans to travel until some later date.

I asked Mum if I could have some good news to tell everyone and she said, "I haven't finished yet, Bridget. Those pains in your legs and both thighs mean that you need two new hip replacements." After a few moments of being shocked I attempted to joke with her by saying, "Does that mean I am always going to have every condition that Dad had?"

My father had been an insulin-dependent diabetic, which I am also. Dad had also suffered and been crippled by arthritis in his later years, and I had seen him in so much pain that his daily life was severely restricted.

Mum said, in response to my question, "Yes. You are like your father in every way except that in his day, he had to suffer the pain unless you gave him healing."

I didn't want to disbelieve Mum so I took her advice and visited a doctor who was standing in for my regular physician. I mentioned my symptoms to him and he just told me that it was nothing to do with my hips.

Mum told me to seek further advice so I did.

I have now seen an orthopedic consultant who informed me that I need two new hips as I have no cartilage between my ball and socket joints on both sides.

Mum also told me that my first operation would be in November, but when I saw the consultant on November 2 at the Calderdale Royal Hospital, he said that there was a four-month waiting list, so it would be at least February or March before I could have the operation. I could hear Mum telling me that he was wrong. "Just wait and see," she said. "We will make sure that you don't have to wait long."

When I came into my office on the morning of November 3, a voice mail was waiting for me to say that a date was set for my operation—it was going to be on Monday, November 19, 2012.

Mum was laughing as she reminded me that she was always right.

So I began preparing myself for this operation and, although I knew that I needed the surgery badly, the consultant could not believe that the pain has only just started. He told me that he had not seen hips as bad as mine in a very long time.

Even though I worked in orthopedics when I was a nurse, I must admit that when I saw my x-rays I was shocked to see the proof of the deterioration in both hips. I made plans to have the right hip done first and then a couple of months later the left one would be operated on—so I would be well and fit in the New Year.

Oddly enough, even though I have left the world of nursing, in some ways I am still a part of it because I know most of the staff on the ward that I am going to be on. Even the nurse who was with the doctor had been to see me for a reading many years ago and she started to tell the doctor what I did for a job. The consultant was very interested in my work and he asked me about healings. I told him that I had done healing on myself every day and he told me that that was what was probably helping me to deal with all the pain. He remarked that with all the pain I must be experiencing it must be very difficult to walk. He said that it was obvious that I had great guides and healers in spirit and I told him that I did, especially my father, mum, and brothers. I told him that they visit me every day to reassure me that all will be okay.

The Surgery

On Monday, November 19, 2012, I arrived on the admissions ward at Calderdale Royal Hospital at 7:00 a.m. I was supposed to go to surgery at 8:00 a.m. but because of delays with my notes and blood tests, my operation was postponed until 12:45 p.m. I was taken to ward 8A, the ward I would return to after my operation and I was prepared for surgery. I had to have a drip of sliding-scale insulin due to being a diabetic and then I was left to rest until my time for the surgery came.

Mathew, my eldest son, had put a selection of songs on an iPod for me to listen to during my operation. I had already been informed by the anesthetist that I would be having a spinal epidural and so would be awake during the surgery.

I lay on my bed listening to the music and I sent a message out to my loved ones in spirit, especially my mum and

Johnnie, to let them know that I was in hospital and that I was soon to have my operation.

I very much wanted a sign from them.

I didn't have to wait long as the sixth song I listened to took me by complete surprise when I heard the words "Take Me Home to Mayo." The tears were streaming down my face—they were tears of joy, not sadness. Mathew had informed me that Grandma's songs were somewhere on the iPod. He had told me not to be shocked but there were 742 songs on the iPod and, yet, that song had to be number six. Then I started to wonder what the significance of the number six was. I would later find that I was number six on the operating theatre list and would be in hospital for six days!

By 12:45 p.m. I was in the anesthetic room being prepared for my operation. The anesthetist was a lovely man who explained exactly what he was going to do. He told me that a spinal epidural would make me numb from my breastbone down to my toes and that both legs would also be numb. He reassured me and asked me if there was anything I wanted to know. I did question what would happen if I needed other anesthesia and he told me that would not be necessary, thus putting my worries to rest.

I was laid on my left side with my right hip abducted. I had a moment of clarity and great empathy when I couldn't feel my legs anymore and I pondered how it must be for people who become paralyzed due to an accident or other causes. I knew I would find it very difficult if that were ever to happen to me.

There were many assisting in the operation. By this time I had a blood pressure cuff in check, my heart rate was monitored, and I had a drip in my left arm and a Venlo in my right hand in order for the anesthetist to administer any other drugs that might be required through the operation. Two consultants assisted and although I was aware of what was going on, I managed to drift off to sleep listening to my music. Every so often I was spoken to by a member of the staff to make sure that I was comfortable and that I wasn't feeling any pain. The operation took about an hour and a half and I was taken to recovery and looked after there for at least another hour before I returned to the ward. I knew many of the staff so I felt reassured by that. The anesthetist kept coming back to check to make certain I was okay.

This experience brought home to me that from the time I was in nursing back in the 1990s to today, a great deal has changed. The fact that I was having a major operation that I was awake throughout was incredible. I was constantly reassured during the entire operation and told how everything was going wonderfully. The two consultants who performed the operation did a fantastic job and the anesthetist who kept me pain-free and comfortable at all times was remarkable! I wish to most sincerely thank everyone who assisted both before, during, and after the operation. All the staff on the ward, both day and night, from the housekeeper to the most senior of staff was pleasant and, even though the ward was hectic, every patient was treated with dignity.

After the surgery I had to have a charley wedge placed between my legs to keep me from turning over and that had to stay in place for twenty-four hours. I actually think that was the most uncomfortable part as I always sleep on my side and it seemed a bit different, but I managed to cope with it.

As the week progressed I was up on my second day with the aid of a Zimmer and physiotherapy which I managed quite well. But despite doing okay I couldn't understand why I was feeling so nauseated and then being sick. I thought maybe it was due to the different analgesia (pain medication).

On November 20, I sent out my thanks to the spirit world and to God for giving me such wonderful people to perform my operation. I also asked Mum why I was being so sick. I didn't have long to wait when she came back and said, "You lost a lot of blood during the operation, Bridget, and now you need a blood transfusion."

My first thought was: Oh, no! I am now going to have to have someone else's blood and I wondered who it would belong to.

Mum came back, "A good person, Bridget."

I was concerned because I am a rare blood group and it was important that I was grouped and cross-matched.

I was given two units of blood and by Thursday of that week I was starting to feel like myself again.

By that Saturday I was ready for discharge and came home later that day. I had a peaceful weekend with my family. Kenn, Mathew, Elizabeth, and Marcus were at hand to cater to all my needs and I couldn't have wished for better. I had to get used to using crutches, managing the stairs, and all the things that we take for granted in everyday life. For the first time in my life, I felt trapped and reliant on everyone else instead of it being the other way around.

On November 27, I had a second blood test and it was confirmed by my doctor on Thursday that my blood count was still too low. I was given the choice to either have another blood transfusion or to go ahead with a month's supply of iron supplements, which I chose to do.

Each day I was getting stronger. I returned to see the consultant on January 2, 2013 to check that everything has healed as it should. To me it is totally amazing how my body can cope and adjust so well to having a new part fitted in order for me to be pain-free and mobile again. I am now preparing myself for my second hip operation and I will be told when to expect that after I see the consultant.

Since January 2008 when I lost my lovely sister-in-law, Anne, to a sudden heart attack up to the present, I have undergone a time of loss among my loved ones. After Anne's passing, my brother Charlie (Anne's husband) died of a brain tumor on January 5, 2009. Then came Mum's sudden passing on April 14, 2010. On April 19, 2011, my dear friend

Nicola passed to spirit. On November 25, 2011, my sister-in-law Lisa passed. On May 21, 2012, my brother Johnnie passed.

And now this surgery has happened.

These past years, since Anne's death to now, have taught me great empathy and I truly feel that I have dealt well with all that I have been faced with.

I also have no doubt that many people will question why all this has happened to me in such a short space of time. Knowing that both joy and sorrow come to us all, my reply would probably be that I am no different than anyone else. It is just that I have been blessed with a gift that allows me to communicate with my loved ones in spirit as well as the loved ones of others and this communication gives me a coping skill I am very grateful for.

From all of this I have learned that life is a journey with its trials and tribulations. This thought takes me back to the first time I communicated with spirit when Harry made himself known to me and told me that one day I would be known worldwide. Little did I know that I would be able to reach out to people around the world who were experiencing their own troubles and be able to help them to come to terms with what life was giving them.

⌒⌒

While I know I am blessed to have the gifts that I do, I must say from my heart that it is sometimes very difficult. As I sit here I can vividly recall a day in 1996 when I was returning from a trip to Ireland with my family and saw a young man with red hair getting off a ship and getting on his motorbike. I had this overwhelming feeling that he wasn't going to make it home. I wondered if I should go to him and tell him, but something held me back. No more than a few moments later and about a mile down the road, that same young man was involved in a fatal accident. We passed the accident in our car and I could clearly see that it was him. A lady was just covering his broken body. The entire family saw it and I still think about it to this day. I never knew his name but I had a feeling that there was a mother waiting somewhere for her son to come home. I felt strongly that his father was in spirit as I could clearly see a man in spirit standing next to the young man.

Incidents such as this are very difficult for me. I realize that I cannot alter the future, but I sometimes wonder if I did the right thing by not stopping to speak to the young man.

Other difficult moments come when I talk to a person I do not know and I see that their transition to spirit is imminent. I send out my thoughts to my guides and inspirers as to how I should best deal with this and they tell me they will help with such a trying moment and I am given the strength to answer any questions that are asked of me.

Quite often people that I meet mention my eyes. Many have told me that they feel as though I am able to look straight through them, and perhaps that is the case. The ability to see future events in a person's life brings vision that is beyond the scope of everyday sight, and that is perhaps why the eyes manifest as different from the ordinary. In fact, when I was coming through the airport a short while ago at check-in, the lady that I was dealing with kept looking at my passport and then at me. Just as I was about to board the plane, she approached me and said, "When you came to check-in and you looked at me, you sent a shiver through my body as if I had met you before and yet I have never met you. I made an inquiry and I feel very proud to shake your hand as I have learned in this last half hour a lot about you and I definitely know that we will meet again in private." When I looked at this lady I could see the younger version of me in her.

There was also a young woman who had read my first book, *When Tomorrow Speaks to Me*, and although she was only thirteen years old, she told me that when she read about Lucy, she felt that she was definitely Lucy, and I realized then that she bore a striking resemblance to Lucy as well. When I asked her what she thought about my book, she said that both she and her sixteen-year-old sister couldn't put it down, and that it was "magical" and made them feel that, even though they had known of young people who had lost their lives in tragic circumstances, they would live on the other side happily and that everyone would one day meet up again.

As for the gift of healing that manifested when I was three years old, I now utilize crystals for this purpose and every person who comes through my door for an appointment is told that healing will be given throughout the reading. It should be noted that my gift of healing is not just used for a particular ailment or illness. I would very much like to think that everyone who has ever received healing during the course of a reading received peace, comfort, and a sense of reassurance. If they wish to continue absent or distant healing, I place their name into my healing book where healing is sent out to everyone included at least six times a day, five days a week. I always include healing for all four corners of the world as well as the animal kingdom. I encourage everyone who comes to see me to do the same.

I also give colors for healing and these are the colors of the rainbow. The person and I both visualize a color together and invariably it will be the same color or one very similar. I always ask the person to continue to visualize that color after they have left me in order for the absent/distant healing to continue.

In the midst of comforting and healing, I am also often asked if I have ever encountered any negative spirits. I can say that in all the years of working with spirit, I cannot recall any negativity as all spirits who make contact with me have reached their destination. They always tell me that they would never wish to come back to earth again as they have found eternal peace and happiness.

My gifts have given me great joy and great sorrow. What the public does not see are the tears I shed behind the scenes. My secretary, Julie, who is here in England, is my right-hand person and is often a witness to the aftermath of a tragic reading. My great friend Noreen, in Ireland, sees and helps pick up the pieces. I am so grateful for all the love and support from both of these dear ones in my life as well as that of my family and friends. The journey on our life paths is often not easy and we do as we are called to do. Many times I am asked, "If you have the gift, why are you so affected by earthly conditions?" I answer that question with a question: "If I never feel, then how can I understand?"

I must also say that when I was thinking about the title for this book, the words my mum had said to me from spirit, "Yes, I walk beside you always," as well as the suggestions from spirit, just brought validation that the title should be *We Walk Beside You Always*. From beginning to end of writing this book, spirit has reassured me that they have fulfilled their promise.

We all have or will know the loss of a loved one or a dear pet during our sojourn on earth. I am only one of many who have been given the gift of being able to comfort and help both those transitioning back *home* and those of us who are left behind to continue.

There is great healing and blessing in doing the work I do. And, yes, I know there will always be those in the world who don't believe in the afterlife. But for those like myself who do believe, or have been given the talent to be able to communicate with those who have passed to spirit, we continue with hope and we continue to try and comfort.

I know in my heart that I wouldn't change who I am or what I do for the world.

And knowing that our beloved ones and pets are only a thought away—that death cannot divide us, that life is eternal, and that joyful reunion is a reality—gives me great hope and comfort.

To Write to the Author

If you wish to contact the author or would like more information about this book, please write to the author in care of Llewellyn Worldwide Ltd. and we will forward your request. Both the author and publisher appreciate hearing from you and learning of your enjoyment of this book and how it has helped you. Llewellyn Worldwide Ltd. cannot guarantee that every letter written to the author can be answered, but all will be forwarded. Please write to:

Bridget Benson
⅟ Llewellyn Worldwide
2143 Wooddale Drive
Woodbury, MN 55125-2989

Please enclose a self-addressed stamped envelope for reply, or $1.00 to cover costs. If outside the U.S.A., enclose an international postal reply coupon.

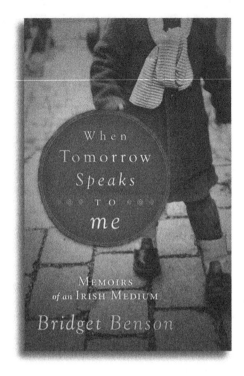

When
Tomorrow
Speaks
TO
me

MEMOIRS
of an IRISH MEDIUM

Bridget Benson

When Tomorrow Speaks to Me
Memoirs of an Irish Medium
Bridget Benson

Tragic deaths, secret love affairs, and powerful messages
from the spirit world have colored Bridget Benson's life. She
grew up in the small Irish farming village of Straide, County Mayo, a county of lush meadows and peat bogs, purple
heather-clad moorland, and sandy-beached lakes. Bridget
lived with her eight siblings, parents, grandparents, and
great aunt in a house with no electricity or running water.
When her grandma died on her seventh birthday, Bridget
received a message that her beloved father, who also had
"the gift," would die when she was twelve years old, and that
she would carry on as the family seer.

When Tomorrow Speaks to Me tells the story of Bridget
Benson's remarkably spiritual life, from her childhood
experiences with spirit guides, ghosts, fairies, and leprechauns to the development of her career as a successful full-time medium.

978-0-7387-2106-4, 240 pp., 5 ³/₁₆ x 8   **$15.95**

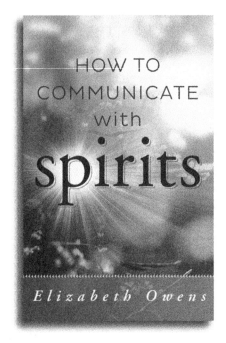

HOW TO
COMMUNICATE
with
spirits

Elizabeth Owens

How to Communicate with Spirits
Elizabeth Owens

Nowhere else will you find such a wealth of anecdotes from noted professional mediums residing within a Spiritualist community. These real-life psychics shed light on spirit entities, spirit guides, relatives who are in spirit, and communication with all of those on the spirit side of life.

You will explore the different categories of spirit guidance, and you will hear from the mediums themselves about their first contacts with the spirit world, as well as the various phenomena they have encountered.

—Noted Spiritualist mediums share their innermost experiences, opinions, and advice regarding spirit communication
—Includes instructions for table tipping, automatic writing, and meditating to contact spirits
—For anyone interested in developing and understanding spiritual gifts

978-1-56718-530-0, 216 pp., 5³/₁₆ x 8 $12.95

MICHAEL NEWTON, PH.D.

JOURNEY
OF
SOULS

CASE STUDIES OF
LIFE BETWEEN LIVES

Journey of Souls
Case Studies of Life Between Lives
MICHAEL NEWTON

Now considered a classic in the field, this remarkable book was the first to fully explore the mystery of life between lives. *Journey of Souls* presents the first-hand accounts of twenty-nine people placed in a "superconscious" state of awareness using Dr. Michael Newton's groundbreaking techniques. This unique approach allows Dr. Newton to reach his subjects' hidden memories of life in the spirit world after physical death. While in deep hypnosis, the subjects movingly describe what happened to them between lives. They reveal graphic details about what the spirit world is really like, where we go and what we do as souls, and why we come back in certain bodies.

978-1-56718-485-3, 288 pp., 6 x 9   **$16.95**

PATRICK MATHEWS

NEVER SAY GOODBYE

A Mediums' Stories of
Connecting with Your Loved Ones

Never Say Goodbye
A Medium's Stories of Connecting With Your Loved Ones
PATRICK MATHEWS

The end of physical life does not have to mean the end of a day-to-day relationship with the people we love. Renowned medium Patrick Mathews reveals that we don't have to let go of family and friends on the other side—in fact, they benefit as much from ongoing communication as we do.

Along with a treasury of heartwarming, compelling, and sometimes humorous true stories from his work as medium, Mathews provides answers to the questions he is most often asked about life in Heaven. *Never Say Goodbye* will help you learn how to recognize spirit communication and establish an ongoing relationship with those in spirit through simple meditations and other practices.

978-0-7387-0353-4, 216 pp., 6 x 9　　　　　**$15.95**

PATRICK MATHEWS

Author of the Bestselling *Never Say Goodbye*

FOREVER WITH YOU

Inspiring Messages of Healing & Wisdom
from Your Loved Ones in the Afterlife

Forever With You

Inspiring Messages of Healing & Wisdom from Your Loved Ones in the Afterlife

PATRICK MATHEWS

After the phenomenal success of *Never Say Goodbye*, Patrick Mathews became one of the most recognized mediums in the country. *Forever With You* invites us back for a closer look at his fascinating life as a spirit communicator and all he's learned.

These vivid and unforgettable stories help us understand what it's like to talk to spirits, how our loved ones have—and haven't—changed since crossing over, and how they continue to impact our lives. Answering questions only a medium can, Mathews offers insight into life's biggest mysteries—what happens when we pass into spirit, heaven and hell, God and angels, reincarnation, the purpose of our physical life, and more.

978-0-7387-2766-0, 240 pp, 5³/₁₆ x 8   **$15.95**